INVISIBLE MEN

GEORGE VICTOR

is a psychoanalytically oriented
clinical psychologist. He practices
psychotherapy in New Jersey and
lectures in psychology at Caldwell
College.

INVISIBLE MEN
Faces of Alienation

GEORGE VICTOR

PRENTICE-HALL, INC., Englewood Cliffs, New Jersey
A SPECTRUM BOOK

Library of Congress Cataloging in Publication Data

VICTOR, GEORGE.
    Invisible men: faces of alienation.

    (A Spectrum Book)
    Bibliography: p.
    1. Alienation (Social psychology) I. Title.
HM291.V44   301.6′2   73-17052
ISBN 0-13-504639-4
ISBN 0-13-504621-1 (pbk.)

A SPECTRUM BOOK

Printed in the United States of America

10 9 8 7 6 5 4 3 2 1

PRENTICE-HALL INTERNATIONAL, INC. (*London*)
PRENTICE-HALL OF AUSTRALIA PTY., LTD. (*Sydney*)
PRENTICE-HALL OF CANADA, LTD. (*Toronto*)
PRENTICE-HALL OF INDIA PRIVATE LIMITED (*New Delhi*)
PRENTICE-HALL OF JAPAN, INC. (*Tokyo*)

Contents

Preface

Oedipus said, "I will speak as a stranger," in dealing with the crime that plagued the community. As a newcomer, unacquainted with the events and people involved, he felt that he could serve as an agent of justice, free of any preconception or conflict of interest. The irony of his dedication was that he himself was the criminal. The "dark things" that he promised to uncover were hidden in his own mind.

A related idea came to me in working on this book. When I began to gather material for it, I had no conscious hypotheses about the nature or causes of alienation. Ideas presented below came to me as fresh insights, and even now many of them seem original. The myth of Oedipus has been reinterpreted here and applied to modern life in a way that departs from traditional psychonalytic thought, and the concept of "Jocasta mothering" was only recently formulated by Besdine (Chapter 2). And there is no comparable psychological analysis of psychopathic behavior and gambling (Chapters 4 and 5). On the other hand, many of my "discoveries" turned out to be rediscoveries of experiences long forgotten. I was a teenager when I first read *The Golden Bough,* and most of us were younger still when we learned about the gods of Greece and Norway and the Knights of the Round Table, the shining heroes of mythology and fairy tale. It was as children that we were fascinated by the heroes' antisocial counterparts—Robin Hood and other tricksters and the evil Mr. Hyde. Our own personal experiences in the role of the most intriguing of Greek heroes—Oedipus—are fragmented memories. For those who have forgotten these elements of our cultural and personal heritage, this book may be a voyage of rediscovery.

Even when we have known alienation ourselves, we approach the study of it as strangers because we are out of touch with the history of our subject. We tend to see alienation as a new phenomenon. Writer after writer proclaims this as the age of alienation. Some of their observations are discussed in Chapter 1, although no systematic comparison with prior ages is available to justify setting ours apart. What is clear is that artists and adolescents and the rest of us are more conscious and articulate about alienation than before. However, our consciousness of it is egocentric and isolated. We forget, when not reminded, about alienation in the past; yet alienation goes back at least to ancient Greece and Israel, although its form and visibility have varied in different cultures and times. For example, in past decades the alienation of introverts was obvious to people, while extroverts seemed fully involved with life. Then Sinclair Lewis made *Babbitt* a part of our vocabulary: the typical extroverted American whose conventionality and smugness hide his extreme alienation even from himself.

Some earlier descriptions of alienation remind us of our own. For example, in fifteenth-century France, Deschamps complained (Urick, 1970):

Why are the times so dark/ Men know each other not at all . . . Deep gloom and boredom . . ./ I know no more where I belong.

Similarly, in 1841 Emerson (1892) found, "A new disease has fallen on the life of man." It is characterized by melancholy and "ennui." (He borrowed the French word, now part of our vocabulary, because he found none in English to describe the condition.) Men care little about life and reject their own identity; they are tormented by "Unbelief, the Uncertainty as to what we ought to do; the distrust of the value of what we do. . . ." They want desperately to be employed, active, accomplishing great things, but are paralyzed and "find it the worst thing about time, that we know not what to do with it." By contrast, Emerson believed that men of earlier times had "planted their foot strong, and doubted nothing."

Emerson seems to have been mistaken about his ancestors; the American heritage is a particularly alienated one. Our colonists were adventurers, criminals, malcontents, religious dissidents, and other wanderers, like some described in later chapters. After a period of settlement, many became restless, leaving the populated East for the open West. The wandering pioneer, isolated prospector, and grim cowboy became images of American manhood. We wrote songs and made jokes about the lonesome cowboy—homeless, unemotional, more comfortable with animals than with people—who remains a model of masculinity. With the disappearance of the western frontier, the city loomed as the place of opportunity; people left their farms to join the urban dispossessed. Then the suburb took form as a promised land and in turn disappointed many who yearned to become part of a community. While these Americans wandered in flight and hope from one part of the country to another, new populations of dispossessed were arriving. The uprootedness of slaves, exiles, and refugees was obvious, but all immigrants are strangers.

Thus many of our fathers were restless, homeless men. And when we remember them as steady, self-assured people, knowing who they were and what they were doing, we may be saying only that we have not known our fathers. Wolfe's (1929) question is addressed to us all: "Which of us has looked into his father's heart? . . . Which of us is not forever a stranger and alone?" When Klapp (1969) and Wheelis (1958), like many who write about alienation, describe their fathers' generation as having no identity problems, we may wonder how fully they have known their fathers.

As Wolfe suggested, estrangement from our fathers may be a cause of our alienation. Not knowing them is also a handicap in trying to deal with it. When we see ourselves as different from our ancestors, we cut ourselves off from the insights they had about their condition.

Alienation is part of our inheritance. The search for identity has been a major theme of fiction since classical Greece. Although the term "alienation" only recently became part of our vocabulary through the writing of Karl Marx, the phenomenon of alienation has been described over and over in the literature with which we grew up.

I have tried to use the past by combining images of man from mythology and classic drama with insights derived from psychoanalytic work. The result is a picture—an arrangement of data and interpretations that is illustrative rather than demonstrative. Occasionally, as in analyzing the role of the hero, I have tried to give a comprehensive view, but even there material has been selected and interpreted to fit. My treatment of material is clinical rather than scientific. I have tried to depict individuals and to illuminate their condition. It is my impression that these pictures fit many people, but they are not intended as a general or comprehensive interpretation of the groups of people referred to.

Case material may seem like objective data, but it is not. A patient selects and distorts what he tells his therapist, and the material undergoes further transformation as it is fitted into an article or book. Finally, identifying data is altered to protect the privacy of the patient.

The above limitations, derived from my choice of material and manner of analyzing it, are hopefully offset by the vividness of the resultant picture. But there is a limitation for which I can only offer regret. This book is primarily about sons. It is also about mothers and their role in the development of their sons' alienation. The alienation of daughters has been neglected, as has the contribution of fathers to alienation in children. This bias is partly a reflection of the sources available. Psychology, sociology, mythology, philosophy, and drama have had much more to say about sons than daughters. Whether men and women are similarly alienated is a difficult question. The role of hero and the alienating processes described below are more available to (or thrust upon) boys than girls in our culture. However, there are other alienating processes (like marriage) whose impact is greater on girls than boys. To try to include women and their alienation in a book largely about men would have more disadvantages than advantages.

In discussing the fostering of alienation in children, I have stressed a theory that involves "Jocasta mothering." Besdine, the theory's author, remarked that a "Jewish mother" need not be Jewish or a mother or even female; the same applies to a Jocasta mother. The parental behavior considered alienating is engaged in by fathers as well as mothers, but in the context of American culture and typical (middle-class) family structure considered below, it would appear that mothers suffer the oppression and engage in the behavior associated with Jocasta more than fathers do.

I am grateful to the following people for encouragement, suggestions, and manuscript criticism: Mary Allen, Sidney Birnback, Miriam Blackman, Elisabeth Brandt, Lewis Brandt, Muriel Dollar, Ugo Giannini, Howard Gruber, Margo Lichtenberg, Colette Lindroth, James McMahon, Stephanie Robinson, Theodore Simms, and Irene Williams. In addition to doing the above, Michael Hunter, Benjamin Lichtenberg, Ammon Roth, and Janice Victor, my wife, discussed many of the ideas with me and were helpful at a number of stages along the way.

□ 1. THE SYNDROME OF ALIENATION

It was not a case of amnesia. A physician whose youth was fading suddenly left his home and practice, his wife, children, friends, and colleagues. He traveled across the country to places he did not know, taking one job after another, wandering, hoping somewhere to find himself. The reason for his odyssey, he said, was the realization that he had been living a false life—in the years he had played the role of successful doctor he had lost himself. His story was presented on television as part of a series on American life.

Experiences like his have been called identity crises. The physician's pathetic wandering and the urgency of his search underline the extremity of his estrangement from himself. When he left home his alienation became visible; people could see it and discuss it, and he could try to do something about it. Earlier he had been no less alienated. He had, as he said, been acting a role; but he had done it so well that even he was often unaware of its artificiality.

When we think of the alienated we are apt to have in mind those who are confused, detached, wandering, or homeless, and we usually forget those who go through the motions of life as if they know who they are and what they are doing. When they fit into the conventions of our culture, as the physician did for a while, we do not question

1

them. Thus many people who are alienated from themselves go unnoticed. The ones who attract our attention and study are those who obviously do not fit—those who are alienated from others and society, like the people to whom later chapters are devoted.

In terms of the ideas developed within this book, alienation from self is a tragic condition,* even though it seems common enough to be considered normal. For those who are severely alienated the loss is usually obvious. Their feelings range from apathy to grinding despair. A few find ecstasy but not fulfillment. Many live apparently ordinary lives until, with advancing years, there comes a deepening sense of a missed chance, of a wasted existence. Others die young by adopting lives of violence or by deliberate suicide. Still others spend a large part of their lives in institutions. The process of alienation touches many in addition to the principal sufferer; near relatives and distant bystanders may pay a price for one person's frustration or destructiveness. When the physician embarked on his lone search, his wife and children were deprived in an obvious way. But they had already been paying the more insidious price of living with the shadow of a man.

A person undergoing an identity crisis is intensely and painfully aware of his condition, and therefore motivated to change. He may visit a psychotherapist, undertake a journey, or strike out violently. Whatever he does can provide an opportunity for him to enlarge his understanding of himself and for others to learn from him. The homeless physician teaches us not only about people in crisis, flight, and search; he gives us clues about what he was like before he left home and about what we are like.

Some of the experiences of alienation described in this book are drawn from patients because of the availability of detailed psychological information. But patients are not necessarily more alienated than nonpatients; in my experience the two groups overlap more than they differ. Patients, however, are more likely to be both acutely conscious of identity problems and eloquent in describing them.

The most alienated person I have seen in recent years was Alan, a college student who often felt as if he were wandering in a surrealistic

---

* My theoretical assumptions are grounded in Western culture, where man is defined as an active, autonomous unit, separate from his environment. Westerners stress individuality. Self-alienation may have different meanings in Oriental cultures, for example, where individuality is minimized and people are seen as members of a larger unity.

daze. He found his life lonely and meaningless, with nothing to look forward to. The world seemed an empty wasteland to him, "a deep existing void." Reading Camus, he identified strongly with *The Stranger*, and saw himself as living on the "fringes of the feeling world, an observer rather than a participant."

At times he was sensitive to the feelings and fantasies of others, but he felt close to no one. He identified no more with students or with people of his own age than with others. Sometimes being with people made him feel even less human, more out of contact than he usually felt. Most of us have moments when we feel like Alan. Like him, we sometimes laugh when we are not amused, even when we feel desolate. But for him desolation was a daily experience.

His mother had died when he was twelve, and his father had remarried for what seemed to Alan simply convenience. It was then that he lost the sense of having a home. "I felt like a stranger . . . it felt like a boarding house." It had seemed to Alan that the others in the family had no feelings for anyone, using each other as handy objects and not minding being used that way themselves. Indifference was a way of life for them. In later years when he too began to experience indifference, Alan felt unnerved. Unlike *The Stranger* and unlike the "cool generation," he had not yet become used to indifference, and the adaptive value of being unaware of emotions did not sufficiently compensate him for feeling less alive.

Alan had been a troubled child long before his mother's death. Afterward, his unhappiness grew deeper, with occasional periods of severe depression, a few a year by the time he sought help. During those periods he gave up his already limited social contacts, not going to class, staying in his room, and ruminating about dramatic resolutions of his life. He often imagined driving in congested areas at high speed in the expectation of an accident or of a fatal encounter with police. On rare occasions he put this idea into operation but, although he drove fast, there were no incidents.

One need not be a patient to feel like Alan, nor need one be eccentric to experience life and self as frustratingly devoid of meaning or to seek unusual and violent remedies. Writer after writer sees modern man, beneath the mask of his bustling activity and consumption of goods, as among the most abject in history in terms of his inner life. In a study of college youth, Keniston (1965) found mental images of "disintegration, decay, and despair." According to Tinder (1964), modern man's thought is dominated by personal isolation and universal meaninglessness, his mood is one of melancholy and terror, and he realizes himself only in negation.

Even if these comments are exaggerated, alienation is very much with us. We talk of it, our news features it, and it has been the dominant theme of serious and prophetic creativity in the last hundred years. Major movements in the arts are particularly expressive of fragmentation, isolation, meaninglessness, and unreality in man's experience, as seen in dadaism, expressionism, surrealism, and abstraction. Alienation has been a major theme in the literature of Joyce, Eliot, Orwell, Huxley, Strindberg, Ibsen, Pirandello, Betti, Moravia, Sartre, Camus, Giraudoux, Anouilh, Hesse, Kafka, Brecht, O'Neill, Tennessee Williams, Arthur Miller, Sinclair Lewis, Nathanael West, Fitzgerald, Hemingway, Dreiser, and, of course, Dostoyevsky. This list is deliberately long to emphasize the point; yet anyone could add to it. Moreover, our serious contemporary theater is increasingly a "Theatre of the Absurd."

The strident, anguished cries of artists and writers gain our admiration and attention, but we react with a curious detachment, like that made fashionable by our "cool" youth, neither laughing nor crying. We sit in silence at dramas, applaud conventionally at the end, and then go home. On television, laughter and applause are often supplied by the program, and even less is asked of us. We, the audience, the mass of men, are approaching a condition defined by Albee (1960) in which "We regard each other with a mixture of sadness and suspicion, and then we feign indifference. . . ."

If detachment is becoming so extreme and common among us, we may be approaching a turning point in the history of man. Philosophers have long stressed the social aspect of man as essential. Aristotle (1943) defined man as a social, political animal, and argued that any individual who "is unable to live in society, or has no need because he is sufficient for himself, must be either a beast or god. . . ." For the Romans, the verb "to live" meant to be among men (Arendt, 1958).

Through the centuries, evidence in support of the aptness of these definitions of man has been seen in the stories and myths of children growing up in the wilderness or locked away from human contact and as a result becoming subhuman monsters. Modern clincal data have supported this idea; infants (usually foundlings) who were reared in institutions with limited social contact have mostly died or failed to mature into whole adults. If this line of argument is valid, a society that is strongly alienating may foster the development of a new, less social type of man—perhaps one who will better fit into the technologically organized future society pictured in our science fiction.

The estrangement and despair to which modern artists point are understood to be woven deeply into our culture, although there is a tendency to think of them as being located largely in the youth subculture, as if only youth suffered this psychic affliction. Such thinking is, as I will argue below, a reflection of our tendency to place young people in a sacrificial role. We venerate them but also blame them for society's problems and expect them to devote themselves to solutions. Thus youth have been blamed in recent years for a decline in the desirability and meaningfulness of work and duty, for changing sex and marriage patterns and a concomitant decline in social cohesiveness and family life, for a growing attitude of nihilism, for the waning legitimacy of institutions and leaders, and for crime generally. But it is paradoxical to blame youth in a society which has been growing to accept the idea that rearing shapes character, that children do what they have been conditioned to do.

It may not be true that youth are our most alienated group (and it may easily be argued that aged people are more so), but they seem to be most visibly, dramatically alienated. Youth exemplify the predicament of not knowing oneself. When we think of alienation we tend to look at youth, and our view is colored by a half-conscious notion that youth's unhappiness and dissent are outcroppings of a timeless Oedipal war between fathers and sons. Feuer (1969), for example, argued that dissident student movements in all ages and cultures have been expressions of such conflict. Similarly Roiphe (1971), writing for the broad audience of newspaper readers, referred to the nuclear family unit as "the source of the alienated, bomb-throwing society." And she offered no explanation, as if none were needed and most readers would intuitively grasp the idea that the family structure of father, mother, and child is what fosters alienation and violence.

Ideas about youth seem to reflect an ancient, deeply held idea: sons are natural enemies of fathers and of society, and without strict rearing (repression) the destructive emergence of their instincts is to be expected. In analyzing family relationships, the ancients focused on the son, passing their ideas on to us mostly through mythology and drama in which parents play secondary roles. From early times we have inherited a way of looking at the family without looking closely at parents.

THE SEARCH FOR RELATEDNESS

The idea that alienation is a feature of our culture and as such provides an alienating context for youth has been discussed in a number of books (for example, Ruitenbeek, 1965); comments here will be limited to only a few aspects of our culture. Social isolation in America is not always evident; on the contrary, our country gives an appearance of closeness and cohesiveness that is remarked on by foreigners. But sometimes the very things that produce this appearance contribute to fragmentation and detachment. It is often said that we are a nation of joiners. A typical college graduate may be a member of his alumni group, his college fraternity and a community fraternal organization, a church, a P.T.A. or other civic group, some professional societies or businessmen's associations, book clubs and other consumer groups, a "Y," country club, or swim club, and a political party. The fact that he may be no more than a passive dues-payer in most of them will not necessarily preclude his feeling a vague threat or loss if any of his memberships lapse. But the very number of clubs and societies he joins may suggest his loneliness and his lack of devotion to any of them. Underneath our joining and busyness is a longing which is pathetic because it does not lead to fulfillment.

In our search for relatedness we are also turning to sex. Intercourse is becoming a means for combating loneliness, for producing moments of wedlock. It used to be traditional for an unattached man and woman to go to dinner or the theater and to try to converse—to try to create or at least simulate a relationship—before going to bed together. Recently, however, as eating and talking together and other elements of dating are becoming less meaningful, people rush into bed to find proof there of some kind of human relatedness. Many patients refer to the act of intercourse (usually limited to a matter of minutes) by saying, "We had a relationship."

People who are frustrated in personal relationships often seek compensation in the possession and consumption of material goods. Ours is a materialistic society; it has been said that we traditionally put property rights ahead of humane goals. But the satisfaction we get from property is only momentary. Marx (1964) distinguished between things possessed for their intrinsic value and those possessed as a means to an end, the latter being an alienating kind of possession. We possess few things for their intrinsic value. Today an American buys a house (usually his principal possession) not to grow attached to it, not to shape it to his individual character, and not as an enduring home. He can expect to live in it about five years and he is more like a tenant in it, aware that he will soon be moving on. Its marketability is a major factor in the repairs and improvements he makes on it. He plants shrubs and trees which will not mature and bear fruit for him or his children. In some communities, the marketability of his house depends on his keeping it nondescript; the more it resembles the average, the easier it is to sell.

Man grows less and less identified with his acts as well as with his property. Alienation from work is most often mentioned. Industrialization and increasing technology have already fostered the breed of specialists who excel at some functions and are not expected to perform others. Individuality, finding less acceptance in technologically organized activities, is replaced by specialization. But the specialist is apt to be a different sort of person than the individual; he tends to lack individual identity and responsibility.

The specialist is identified as a member of a team and a step in a process. The team is the actor or producer. The more diversified the process and the more complex the organization of the team, the less each specialized member is identified with the resultant service or product. (In some instances the specialist does not see the product of his work or the client of the service, and he may not even know what or who they are, nor need he be capable of understanding their nature. In a sense, he does not know what he is doing.)

This picture, with its Marxian assembly-line images, applies increasingly to life in general. The affluent civilization brings more and more of the environment under control, while its citizens singly become less able to deal with it, thus becoming more dependent on other specialists. Primitive man took care of his own and his children's needs for food, shelter, clothing, companionship, entertainment, and education. Modern, affluent man is growing to depend on craftsmen, decorators, lawyers, accountants, advisors, agents, procurers, and arrangers—a battery of people and computers who sample, digest, or select for him wines, books, plays, news, tours, colleges, careers, jobs, candidates, and mates.

In the past, poets and philosophers agreed that "Beauty is truth, truth, beauty." Trilling (1955) interpreted Keats' words as meaning that sensuality and validity are inseparable, that pleasure "is at the root of existence, and of knowledge, and of the moral life." In other words, we learn by our sensual experiences; we learn facts and principles from the gratifications and disappointments we experience. But modern man is in poor contact with the sensual and subjective side of himself, his emotions and basic impulses. Often he does not know or trust what he feels, and like a scientist, he seeks objectivity and facts on which to base his actions and values.

QUESTION: What were your feelings when the President announced the invasion of Cambodia?

ANSWER: Well, there were the enemy bases, and this was an attempt to destroy them.

QUESTION: Yes, but what were *your feelings?*

ANSWER: I felt that the operation had a fair chance of success.

QUESTION: No, no, no! I want to know what your emotions, your body reactions were when you heard the news.

ANSWER: Oh . . . I remember a tightening in my stomach. I think I was anxious.

Emotions come last, if at all. Modern man is not comfortable with the statement, "Truth is beauty." He is more likely to follow the engineer and say, "Truth is what works." A correct idea is one that is successful when applied—"Truth is efficiency."

In line with this creed, people are seen as raw material to be shaped (manufactured, manipulated) into what will work or sell. High school students are commonly called "college material" and treated as such, with parents and teachers collaborating to shape them so that they will satisfy the requirements of colleges. (The reverse idea, that schools should be shaped and pliable to meet the individualized needs of their students, still sounds revolutionary and evokes images of chaos.) The businessman's approach to personal success, "You've got to sell yourself," used to mean emphasizing one's strengths. Presumably a person knew himself and what his strong points were. Now he effaces himself and tries to simulate whatever is marketable. Fromm (1955) used the term "marketing personality" to describe a person who has no character that is distinctly his own but is always ready to play the role that those who are around him expect. In becoming chameleon-like, man has passed beyond being influenced or manipulated by strong forces around him to a stage of self-manipulation.

The predicament of early man, at the mercy of powerful, unpredictable forces of nature, turning to gods and ritual, seemed difficult enough. But now, having gained reasonable mastery of nature, man's predicament seems worse. To a large extent he is master of distance and climate; he has minimized the threats of flood, storm, drought, and his biological enemies. No longer dependent on nature or on the whims of gods, he can synthesize food, clothes, building materials, and even replacement parts for his body as well as his psychological style or role. Yet he feels less in control of his life than did his predecessor. To be a stranger in an alien, threatening place is difficult but acceptable. To be a stranger among one's family, in one's home, in one's own room, and in one's own heart can be devastating.

ALIENATED REMEDIES
FOR ALIENATED CONDITIONS

Wars have the effect of mending the seams of a society as well as facilitating fragmentation and revolution. The phenomena of alienation and apartheid between generations and classes, of which we are so much aware now and identify with the period following World War II, took form before the war. But painters and writers were not, then, seen as speaking for the public. Now we feel closer to our writers —to their own struggles as well as to the struggles of the characters they create. We are less inclined to emphasize distinctions between literary characters and actual people; we even analyze the motives of characters as if they were real, sometimes conscious of the fact that we are doing it to understand ourselves. We are more conscious of rumblings from underground, rumblings from our inner selves as well as from poets and madmen.

Along with our growing awareness of personal and social isolation, we have been turning increasingly to countermeasures, but with little realism. "Togetherness" was promoted to the American people after World War II in so shallow a manner as to be laughable. Many would agree with Tinder (1964) that "togetherness" was not merely superficial but contributed to estrangement. Similarly, exhortations to pray and to attend church probably speeded disaffection from religion, and the habit in the movie and advertising worlds of casually using terms of endearment spread to the public, but became an irritant. Casual endearment had the effect of raising people's hopes toward a new series of disappointments. There is bitterness in the once-popular song:

You call ev'rybody darling . . .
You don't mean what you're sayin',
It's just a game you're playin' . . .*

The song goes on to suggest that one who makes a game out of sweet words will not experience love and will find himself alone.

These cures were themselves symptomatic; they were alienated approaches to alienation. To counter detachment, they offered the appearance of relatedness, completely bypassing the seat and substance of the problem. They were gimmicks, and added to the problem of alienation by hiding its presence and by promoting pretense and synthetic formalism in personal situations. In addition, these counter-measures involved treating people as if they were alike. People were advised to get together without regard for individual interests, moods, or tastes. People were told to go to church whether or not church happened to fit their spiritual growth or state of mind on any particular Sunday, and everybody could be called "darling" when "darling" no longer referred to a genuine feeling. In this day when identity is problematic, when one's sense of individuality and personal responsibility are not clear and have to be struggled over, conformity pressures often have the opposite effect of what is intended.

It is a sign of our time that people send their personal problems by mail (as if the problems were detachable) to strangers to handle for them, to newspaper and magazine columnists who will resolve them out of sight and out of context by reference to some common denominator of the periodical's readers. And article after article, book after book, offers readers a synthetic, packaged, stylized and instant personality. We are offered *standard ways* to practice being sincere, intimate, and even spontaneous.

Togetherness has reappeared as a formal psychological technique. Quasi-therapeutic encounter groups and the use of encounter techniques in psychotherapy are intended to overcome interpersonal barriers. In addition, discussion-encounter groups are used to overcome division between groups in a community. Physical touching, with or without nakedness, has become the road to contact and intimacy. One therapist encouraged his patients to develop trust in him by having them walk blindfolded on the parapet outside his window while hold-

---

* *You Call Everybody Darling*. Lyrics and music by Sam Martin, Ben Trace, and Clem Watts. New York: Mayfair Music Corp. © Copyright 1946 by Edwin H. Morris & Co., Inc. Used by permission.

ing his hand. Other therapists have reversed the technique, placing their own well-being in the hands of their patients. Many therapists (as well as laymen) employ drugs to dissolve barriers to communication. There is no question about the effectiveness of the settings and techniques used for fostering a quick feeling of intimacy between strangers. We have long known of situations in which people are thrown together with facilitating effects. The question is, when the session is over are there enduring effects? Is intimacy with oneself and the people in one's daily round increased? Or does the encounter session become distinguished as a *special place in which it is safe to act freely,* comparable to a bar, ship, or convention? Have we established another setting for brief encounters which emphasize the alienation of the intervening periods of ordinary life?

The data are not yet in, and it is surely too early to judge how this form of contact will develop in the future. But the pressure for fast results—instant intimacy—is not encouraging. Some of the original T-groups or sensitivity sessions—precursers of the encounter—were designed to become a part of the lives of the participants. Their members were people who worked together and would continue to react to each other in their daily lives after the special sessions. But the trend has been for encounter groups to become occasional gatherings of unrelated people who will not pursue whatever beginnings are generated with each other.

VARIETIES OF ESTRANGEMENT

The word "alienation" has been used in such varied contexts and ways that it has many meanings. Sociologists interested in the relationship between man and society have devoted considerable analysis to people with detached and hostile orientations toward society.* This group sometimes arouses more animosity than sympathy in the viewer. MacIver (1950), for example, warned against the

> . . . *state of mind of one who has been pulled up by his moral roots, who has no longer any standards but only disconnected urges, who has no longer any sense of continuity, of folk, of obligation . . . spiritually sterile, responsive only to himself, responsible to no one. He derides the values of other men. His only faith is the philosophy of denial. He lives on the thin line of sensation between no future and no past.*

---

* Sociologists have used the word "anomie" to describe such people.

This group corresponds approximately to the psychiatric category of psychopaths, who are the subject of Chapter 4.

Seeman's (1959) classification of varieties of alienated experience is among the best known (his descriptions refer to subjective feelings or ideas and not necessarily to objective reality; for example, a person who feels powerless may actually be strong):

> Powerlessness: the expectation that one's behavior cannot determine outcomes
>
> Meaninglessness: lack of clarity about criteria for decision making and inability to predict outcomes
>
> Normlessness (anomie): the expectation that only unapproved behavior may bring desired outcomes
>
> Isolation: not valuing goals or values widely held in society
>
> Self-estrangement: seeing one's acts as of value only in terms of external consequences (rather than intrinsic pleasure or self-satisfaction)

Many more concepts of alienation have been used, and a simple way of summarizing them is to list the things a person may be or feel detached from:

> gods
> nature
> society's rules and values
> community
> other people
> one's emotions and desires
> one's acts
> work
> property
> technology

In addition to detachment, one may feel a lack of:

> power
> life or existence
> guidelines for thought or action
> purpose or direction
> identity or individuality
> place or position

Another way of describing the experience of alienation is in terms of the image that the alienated person has of himself.

A zombie

A computer

A puppet or robot

A performer or gladiator

A greyhound, in hot pursuit of what remains always just out of reach (The performer, puppet, and greyhound often share a feeling that they are exploited.)

An observer or supernumerary (Turgenev [1950] gave a fictional account of a man who saw himself as a fifth horse on a four-horse coach. He felt that he had completed his life journey as a reserve without being used. He was worn out by the trip without contributing to the outcome of anything. Had he not made the journey [not lived], it would have made no difference in anyone else's life. Whatever he had tried to do, wherever he had tried to fit himself in, there had always been someone else ahead of him. In addition he had always felt unnatural and awkward, like the extra horse who was tied to the coach in a special way which compelled him to run stiffly in an arched posture, amusing to others and painful to himself.)

A still different approach to classification involves the ways in which people react to their alienation. Some confront it actively, trying to change themselves or their environment. They pursue self-examination or psychotherapy; they seek people who are like themselves and may join movements, communes, or groups of anonymous alcoholics, drug addicts, and gamblers. Some become revolutionaries, trying to change their environment directly or indirectly (as through pamphleteering or art). And some accept the terms of society while trying to "win," pursuing wealth or prestige in a single-minded way, giving up self and social interests in the process. This group includes devotees of encounters and of mystical disciplines, hippies, student activists and artists, professional soldiers, gamblers and racing drivers, and eighty-hour-a-week executives and physicians. Many of these people are easily identified as alienated.

Some try to ignore their alienation by detaching themselves still further. They become super-cool, resigned, or apathetic. Easy enough to recognize as alienated when something draws them to our attention, they are often forgotten because they tend to be innocuous. They may manage marginal social adjustments or be derelicts, and they number among the drinkers, drug users, dropouts, hermits, and those who are present but only putting in time.

And some disguise their alienation from themselves or others by the appearance of normalcy. They may hold steady jobs and participate in family, social, and community activities. But, doing these things without the foundation of knowing themselves and their relationship to the world, they rely heavily on convention. They adhere to rules, whether of etiquette, custom, morality, or law. Mechanical conformity, without understanding the context of their actions, is their adaptation. They copy what others do. Although the need behind their conformity may be desperate, they lack genuine involvement with people. Their efforts go primarily into appearances.

It is not clear how the above concepts, experiences, and styles of adjustment are connected nor if they are sufficiently connected to apply a single term, "alienation," to them. Many writers consider the variety to be manifestations of a single underlying condition, but that assumption is not yet justified. From here on the focus will narrow to alienation from self, which will be implied when the word "alienation" is used. Other kinds of alienation are derivable from self-alienation, as is suggested below, but only to a limited extent. Thus the book is not comprehensive. The focus here is on people as individuals, with their alienation interpreted in relation to their experiences in growing up. Child-rearing practices vary from one culture to another; thus culture shapes experiences that are shared by many children within a culture. Cultural influences on the rearing of children will be stressed; however, cultural factors in alienation will not be surveyed fully.

Self-alienation is indicated when a person says, "Who am I? Where do I belong? What am I doing?" or when he suggests that he is out of touch with himself without saying so. Self-alienation means a lack of a sense of an inner core which integrates and gives personal meaning to the many traits, emotions, and acts identified with oneself. Self-alienation will include the above-mentioned self-estrangement, detachment from one's emotions, desires, and acts, and seeing oneself as a zombie, computer, puppet, performer, or greyhound.

We can easily identify a person who says, "Who am I?" as being out of touch with himself. But there are those who have succeeded in tailoring themselves to particular roles which they play over and over so well as to convince themselves that the roles *are* themselves. If a person does not feel alienated, if he insists, "I know who I am and where

I'm going," then we have a problem in calling him alienated. Theoretically we could classify such a person as alienated under the following conditions:

> He is extremely dependent on his role and would feel lost or become disorganized or apathetic if unable to continue performing it.
>
> His role is a narrow or superficial one, encompassing only a small fraction of the elements of his personality and life history.

For example, we can call a man alienated if he feels he is himself only when he is playing football. We can consider him alienated if he minimizes or disowns the rest of his life. We might also wonder about someone whose life style seems temporary and highly determined by external factors. Let us imagine a remarried man whose friends are new and were introduced to him by his present wife. He seems to fit well with them and he indicates that they and their recreational pattern of late parties and active sports suit him. But we remember that a few years ago he was married to a home-centered woman and that he used to spend his evenings and weekends around the house. He had seemed entirely content with that life until his wife left him. And we remember him earlier with still another woman and life style. We might infer that he is like an actor who can play whatever role is called for, but that no role is his own.

Thus we might classify a person as alienated if he identifies himself by limited behavior that is largely dependent on external factors. In later chapters such an identification will be discussed as the cause of alienation. In brief, it will be argued that a child, in adopting a narrow role that is given to him by a parent, is conditioned to become unresponsive to elements of himself that are not consistent with the role. He will learn (to the extent that he cooperates with the parent) to ignore his own desires, tastes, or feelings. In other words, he will become externally oriented, other-directed, and not skilled in implementing his most personal needs.

If the child masters his assigned role, he should be able to play it not only for his parent but for others who want it. And to the extent that he fails to develop skills for implementing his own needs, he will have only limited ways to relate to people. That is, he will be able to relate to people who value his special role. What he will be much less able to do will be to relate to people on the basis of his own desires, aversions, or fantasies. To paraphrase Polonius, because he is not true to himself, he will not be able to have genuine friendship with any man.

If his role is a very narrow one, like that of champion athlete, possibilities for performing it will be limited. Assuming that circumstances are favorable and that the community prizes his specialty to the extent that he is in demand and allowances are made for his shortcomings in other respects, he will fit in and will have a clear sense of purpose. His acts will seem meaningful to him and effective. And if his role is revered in the culture, he may feel that he has great power and embodies the ideals of his community. On the other hand, if he fails to attain special status, he will feel isolated, hopeless, and lacking in self, purpose, and power. It will be easier for him if his role is broader, like that of helper or rescuer. There are many ways in which a person can find public acceptance in serving others—many jobs or professions. And the role of helper may also serve as a basis for marriage or other personal relationships insofar as people who are seeking help may be attracted to him.

Total acceptance is rare. More common is limited acceptance that is contingent on achievement. Those who marry a champion or hire one are likely to demand perpetual high performance from him. And he is likely to expect it of himself. Many salesmen, for example, operate under high self-imposed pressure in addition to prodding from superiors. They go through cycles of exaltation and depression. When high, they are full of purpose; when low, life and work seem meaningless and their alienation is apparent. But they may be considered alienated when they are up as well as down. The superstar is defined as alienated to the extent that his sense of self and purpose depend on the performance and acceptance of his special, narrow role.

A FACE IN THE CROWD

The development of self-alienation, arising from the adoption of the role of champion and leading to powerlessness, meaninglessness, and detachment from people, is illustrated in the following history. Ben is a tall, thin man in his middle twenties. He looks awkward and weak, although he was once an athlete. He is highly conventional and identifies with our culture's traditional values. But he is also a dropout. His main concern is the anxiety that hinders him from facing obstacles and taking important steps, particularly in getting into more challenging and higher-paying work. There is only one thing that he would clearly prefer to do—live the life of an athlete—but he gave up the idea as impossible when he failed to make the basketball team in college.

After giving up basketball he began to lose interest in his studies and to drink heavily. Although he missed many days of school and often came to class with a hangover, he managed to escape notice. But he fell further and further behind until he dropped out of school. It was then that he got a job as a clerk, intending it only as a temporary expedient.

Although his job provides security, it does not interest him. There is no other job he would rather be doing, but he has a restless feeling that he should be doing better. From time to time he thinks of something to try; then he wonders if the idea is his own or someone else's. A similar vagueness is characteristic of many of Ben's involvements. He and his wife have no children and he does not know if he wants any or on what basis they could decide whether to have any. Similarly he is not sure how he feels about continuing his marriage. The idea of an affair appeals to him, especially when he is angry with his wife. Yet he has no particular woman in mind. His social life is limited; it centers around Alcoholics Anonymous meetings.

Ben had majored in business with the idea of preparing himself for a struggle to the top in the corporate arena. Such a career was what his mother had long expected of him. But he was drinking and withdrawing so much that he was headed toward institutionalization. Between these alternatives he eventually found a third course, the life of an anonymous self-renouncing alcoholic who conformed to a simple routine. Athletics, success, institutionalization, and A.A. were all paths of alienation.

The experiences that brought Ben to these paths go back to his earliest childhood. He was the first of two children and clearly his mother's favorite. She was an ambitious woman; her home life and husband had never satisfied her. Much of the time she was mildly depressed, and Ben remembers the bad days when she stayed in bed and wept. After Ben's brother was born, she insisted that the family required a higher income and took a job. Ben's father, a mailman with a modest, steady income, had been opposed to his wife's taking the job. Unable to satisfy her or to get her to accede to his wishes, he expressed his growing resentment both indirectly and directly. He frustrated her by holding out an increasing portion of his wages, spending it on drinking and gambling, and he fought with her when he came home drunk. From time to time Ben's mother would say that she was expecting trouble that night and would invite Ben into her bed. The idea was that his presence might inhibit his father's rage and thus protect her. The two of them would lie talking fearfully, knowing more or less that the strategy would not work.

Protection of his mother as a child of seven was not Ben's first special and responsible position. When he was four his mother gave him the job of looking after his brother in her absence. It was a role he accepted, although he found it burdensome and it kept him from playing with other children. When he began school he came home directly each day to resume his responsibilities. He resented his mother for these things and because she worked, yet he accepted her explanation that she could not depend on her husband and that the future of the family depended on Ben's greatest effort.

Thus the role of child was not his for long. Instead of devoting herself to meeting his needs, his mother substantially reversed the situation. She wanted someone in whom she could confide, someone who would comfort and protect her and provide her with hope of a better future. Although she did not provide the family with a prosperous life by taking a job, she did save for her son's education and future success. When Ben went to college, it was with "her money." The dream appealed to Ben. His regrets and resentment over missed pleasures of childhood were balanced by the prospect of a heroic career in which gratification would be his eventually. Ben seems willingly to have suppressed his own inclinations in adopting the role his mother offered.

His role as her hero included the part of platonic lover. Besides mutual admiration, he spent much time in bed with her. During the day, when she lay in bed crying, he came to her to comfort and cheer her. In the evening he lay with her to protect her. It is hardly surprising that he was overstimulated and confused sexually. During his early school years he was preoccupied with sexual fantasies and the guilt which they aroused. Fear that the teacher would notice his erections and discover his fantasies added to his distractions. He barely managed passing grades.

Later his obsessions subsided. He became inhibited sexually and interested in his muscles and his height as basketball became a source of satisfaction and a means for achieving stardom. Less occupied with guilt, he began to get the high grades his mother had always expected of him and to plan for the greatness which she had foreseen.

To summarize Ben's development, since early childhood he had tried to fulfill his mother's expectations. She had wanted more than a child, and in responding to her demands he became precociously competent in many ways. He also became a performer who tried to please teachers and others as he grew older. However he remained frustrated. His own interests were suppressed and he found that he could not fully satisfy his mother. Even when he was doing well, as in his teens, he often felt that he was a failure. Nevertheless he persisted in trying to become a star into his twenties. When he gave up, he was lost—unsure of his purpose and direction, unclear about his wants. He had long been suppressing and disguising his desires and emotions. Now he was aware of little in himself other than anxiety, irritability, and the vestige of a restless urge to excel. In adjusting, in reestablishing a partial sense of self, Ben joined and identified with the self-effacing people who call themselves Alcoholics Anonymous and rely on common purpose rather than individuality as a basis for orienting their lives.

The thesis illustrated by Ben's life is that being chosen as a child for a special, favored, high-status role is conducive more to becoming a performer than an individual. In fitting himself into his role, a child fails to develop himself and becomes dependent on the role. And if he gives it up or loses it, he has little on which to rely in forming relationships with people or in giving meaning to his acts and experiences.

Ben's alienation is not apparent to his acquaintances. People meeting him now would find him neither heroic nor particularly disturbed. He has become an ordinary-appearing person with traces of heroic aspirations. Some people wonder why, with his intelligence, he is not in a more rewarding job. And he thinks he should be doing better. But such circumstances are commonplace, as are restless feelings generally in our culture. Many people are uncertain about their marriages and about having children. Most of us suffer anxiety in anticipation of taking important steps. The man who feels that he should be in a somewhat higher position, earning more money, is Everyman in America. And the conditions of Ben's childhood differ only in degree from a typical cultural pattern described in the next chapter.

□   2. THE HERO

The hero of mythology was typically a young man who did not know his parents or the land of his birth. A foundling, he carried a name strangers had given him. And, because he did not know himself, he was estranged from everyone. Being so cut off and incomplete contributed to his discontent, his restless urge to wander, to discover and change things. Being cut off also made him able to take the risks and accomplish the courageous feats that are the mark of heroes.

Today all of us are cut off from our heritages and ourselves to some extent. Any similarity between us and the hero of myth is not coincidental. The human forces that shaped his image influence our character development. For those like Ben who are very alienated, the resemblance to these heroics is greater. But many of us were born to mothers whose frustration or depression was serious enough to influence our lives, because sexual servitude and frustration has been the general condition of women in our culture. And oppressed people traditionally dream of champions or saviors, children who will redeem them.

If Ben had followed his early academic achievement with success in the business arena, he would have become the hero of his mother's dream. He had already been her champion in other ways: comforting her in times of despair, freeing her from some of the care of his brother so that she could leave the house, and trying to protect her from the aggression of his father. These were things she openly wanted, and he did them. Here the connection between her wish and his behavior is obvious.

Ben also developed traits which, while in the tradition of heroes, were not obviously part of his mother's plan. He sought glory in physical feats (athletics); he developed a style of doing what people asked of him; and he became a lost person, drifting without knowing who he was or what he was to be. It seems likely that some of these developments in him reflected his mother's unspoken needs. But we do not know what her unspoken needs were; we lack the half-conscious and unconscious details of the image of the hero she hoped her son would be. However, we can assume that some of the missing details were not unique and that this mother's fantasy had features in common with fantasies of other mothers in similar situations.

The personalities of heroes and the feats they perform are similar in many parts of the world. Though variations occur from myth to myth, there is enough similarity for us to define a general image of the hero. We have data (below and in Chapters 5 and 6) showing that despairing mothers look to their sons as heroes and that sons who devote themselves to fulfilling their mothers' wishes develop heroic traits, and in doing so become alienated. *The image of the hero is the hypothetical bridge between a mother's wish and her son's character; it is her fantasy and his model.*

Mothers, however, are not the only ones who turn to their sons. Most of us rely on our youth. We use them as soldiers for our protection and aggrandizement, as athletes for our excitement, and as lovers for our inspiration and rejuvenation. We use them vicariously (as in drama) as well as directly. Those who openly say that youth are the main hope of our disintegrating society are expressing what is hidden in the minds of many of us, as we postpone realistic confrontation of our problems and wait for a savior to appear. We imitate youth's style of hair, dress, and speech in the hope of making our lives vital. We are fascinated by youth. It is their violence, their sexuality, their drug use—dramas in their lives, imaginary as well as real—that draw our attention. The ways in which we as a society use youth make the hero and his traditional social role relevant to our attempt to understand the condition of youth and of other alienated people.*

---

* Similarities in the interests of mothers and communities in relation to youth will be explored below; in both cases, the need for a savior leads to the creation of a scapegoat.

A body of related myths contains a theme and a set of variations on it. The theme has often remained constant through centuries of retelling, and thus contains what is common to the thinking of dozens of generations. Myths are not necessarily true psychology; they may or may not tell us what people are like and what they do. But they are relevant to psychology in revealing images and ideas that are deeply woven into cultures, including those less conscious ones expressed in symbolic form. Images and ideas, whether objectively valid or not, influence people's behavior.

In the interpretation of mythical heroes offered below, the climactic period of their lives occurs when they are approaching manhood. It occurs in their search for identity and place, in their ordeals and efforts to overcome obstacles to the attainment of manhood—a period analogous to the painful, protracted adolescence of today. In exploring origins of hero myths, alienation emerges as an essential feature.

Comparison of alienated youth to mythic heroes is not new, but the comparison has not been combined with detailed psychological analysis nor carried far.* In fact, the idea that classic heroes of myth and tragedy were alienated has often been rejected as improper; it has been said that alienation is a modern concept and therefore could not have been used by writers and storytellers of the distant past. However self-alienation is not a new concept; the tradition of interpreting the odysseys of heroes of literature and mythology as searches for identity is well established. Alienation is not new, but its rediscovery is especially timely in an age when man's odyssey seems increasingly critical.

THE LEGEND OF OEDIPUS

The restless wanderer in search of his birthright, his identity, his manhood, and his fate is a familiar figure of world literature. His odyssey was as meaningful to ancient Greeks as it is to contemporary Americans. This hero was always different, whether by birth or temperament, from the mass of men who knew their places and were content to stay in them. Usually a lonely stranger, in his search to find himself he often became involved in the affairs of nations, as-

---

* Slochower's (1961) interpretation of delinquency is a notable exception.

suming the roles of destroyer of institutions and tyrants, violator of taboos, discoverer of truth, and savior of the oppressed.

Of the ancient heroes, the one most often chosen as a model for understanding the journey of modern man is Oedipus. We have extended Freud's use of the Oedipal myth in explaining severe conflict in young boys to interpret the behavior of large segments of our youth —on the college campus and on the streets in times of protest, as well as in the home. Sociological and psychological data are interpreted as showing that America is producing large numbers of Oedipal sons— disturbed youths whose problems with intimacy and authority pose a crisis for our civilization.* Yet the myth of Oedipus remains incompletely studied, and the popular view of it is distorted.

A common interpretation of the myth stresses the idea that Oedipus desired his mother but ignores the idea that she desired him. Even conventional psychoanalytic thought points to a murderous impulse in sons directed at fathers, while fathers' wishes to be rid of sons are underplayed. However in the main extant version of the myth— Sophocles' play—the emphasis is reversed. The mother is portrayed as willing to do almost anything, including defying the gods, because of her inordinate love for her son. And the father is described as having deliberately tried to kill his innocent son. The Western world, which has accorded Sophocles' drama the longest, most honored reception of any play, seems to have forgotten that the ignorant, blundering, and then literally blind Oedipus is the hero of it and not the villain.

The myth is as follows.** Laius and Jocasta, rulers of Thebes, have

---

* Slater (1970), Roiphe (1971), Keniston (1968).

** Classic Greek playwrights, like modern playwrights and psychoanalysts, found myths useful for illuminating the character of man, for revealing hidden determinants of human behavior. There are many versions of the Oedipus myth; the best-known one is followed here, but I have minimized the magical power of the Oracle. Whatever we may conjecture regarding Sophocles' beliefs about gods, oracles, and destiny, it is clear that he employed oracular prophecies and revelations as dramatic devices, manipulating them to suit his own purposes. A psychoanalytic approach would be to take an oracle or seer as a revealer of the unconscious thoughts of those who consult him, and to do so may not be inappropriate to Greek tradition. The Delphic Oracle, the one featured in the play and myth of Oedipus, presented itself to the public under the apt motto, "Know Thyself." And "The ancient Greeks, as Plato reports, believed that we discover truth . . . by 'remembering' . . . searching into our own experience" (May, 1953). *Oedipus Rex* is commonly interpreted as a man's struggle against his destiny, but Heraclitus said, "character is destiny," suggesting that a man's adventures are determined by his character, which in turn is shaped by his prior experiences (Winnington-Ingram, 1968). Oedipus and his mother do search their own memories in the play. She becomes been childless for some time. Seeking help with this problem, they hear a prophecy that they will have a son who will kill his father and marry his mother. To prevent such an outcome, Laius refuses to sleep with his wife. Years pass under these conditions, until Laius impregnates her when drunk (i.e., unwittingly). Later, his fears overriding his yearning for a child, Laius cripples his newborn son and sets him out in the wilderness to die. Thereafter Laius and Jocasta remain childless.

Oedipus, the son, is rescued and given to another childless king and queen who raise him. In adolescence he hears that he is destined to kill his father and have children by his mother. Although he is uncertain about his identity, he does not understand that he is an adopted son. He leaves his home and parents to avert tragedy and to find a different life and fate.

Wandering without direction, he meets Laius but they do not recognize each other. Laius strikes Oedipus, who becomes enraged and kills his father. Continuing his travels, Oedipus unwittingly finds himself in the city of his birth, where he is set upon by the Sphinx, who has been oppressing his people. He responds to her challenge and causes her death, thereby freeing the land. As a reward the hero-savior is enthusiastically offered the hand of the widowed queen. He follows the wishes of the people and becomes king. (Sophocles emphasizes that Oedipus is not the initiator of any of these acts.) Oedipus, who has outdone his father in combat and in serving the people, also ends his mother's barrenness; Jocasta bears several children by him.

However, the good that Oedipus brings to the city ends—a plague occurs and the citizens beg Oedipus to save them again. It is suggested to him that the discovery and punishment of the former king's killer are necessary in order to end the bad times. In ignorance of the implications, Oedipus devotes himself to this mission despite warnings, including those of his wife-mother, that things are better left as they are. Pushing on relentlessly, he unearths the true story of his involvement with his mother and father. Jocasta then commits suicide and Oedipus blinds himself and becomes a wanderer again.

Alienation is the theme of the ending. The hero says that he is no longer willing to look upon his experiences and behavior; he puts

---

alarmed and stops, warning her son that it would be better to remain ignorant. And, although the discovery of the truth comes as a terrible shock, both of them have consciously anticipated it. Oedipus relies in his inquiry on the seer Tiresias, the expert at truths which are distressing and unspeakable (Fergusson, 1949). But Tiresias, somewhat like a psychoanalyst, throws the questions back at Oedipus, reminding him that the answers may be found inside his mind.

his eyes out as a symbol of his rejection of himself. Nor is he willing to associate with people whom he knows. He chooses to live as a homeless stranger. But he has always been one. He had begun life as an outcast; as an adolescent he had been unhappily confused about his identity. He had never sought any particular place or activity; his wandering was aimless, and he took things as they came.

The myth of Oedipus was the subject of many Greek plays and was known also in other cultures. We may wonder why this tortured stranger is found in so many places. Two kinds of explanation will be considered. The content of the myth may be interpreted as a reflection of the circumstances out of which it developed. And the myth may be seen as perpetuated because, like any enduring dramatic fiction, it continues to meet people's personal needs, especially their unrealized desires and fantasies.

Alienation has not been stressed in most familiar psychoanalytic interpretations of the myth of Oedipus. Our culture has substantially adopted the myth as a model for understanding family life and in particular the nature of boys and how they can grow into neurotic young men. However, we have distorted the story by moralizing it, interpreting it to mean that there are dangerous impulses in boys which must be curbed if civilization is to endure. Sophocles' contemporaries had less need to distort the legend. They were close in geography and time to cultures in which killing of kings and incest were accepted.* These subjects, dealt with in drama, were presumably discussed offstage as well. Commentators in later cultures argued that Oedipus offended the gods by his unwitting incest and parricide, and that his condemnation and downfall were inevitable by Greek standards. But Sophocles and his audiences considered the moral question arguable. At the end of *Oedipus Rex* the hero's spiritual status remained pending; in the sequel, *Oedipus at Colonus,* Sophocles vindicated him.

Themes of incest, parricide, and identity confusion are common in mythology and often linked; their function will be clearer after examining hero myths as a class. Similarities of birth and childhood are striking in the legends of the principal heroes of many cultures (for example, Moses, Hercules, Siegfried, Romulus and Remus, Sargon of

---

* Incest was common among Greek gods and in creation myths of many cultures. According to Masters (1963), the prohibition of incest grew in Greece during the Classical Period. But even when forbidden, it was hardly punished. In Homer's version of the myth, which is earlier than Sophocles', there is no punishment of Oedipus. In Persia, mother-son incest was highly regarded. Killing of kings was practiced in many places (see below).

Babylon, Cyrus of Persia, and Karna of India). From a survey of many myths, Rank (1959) abstracted a "standard myth" from which the following is adapted:

> *Parentage.* At least one of the parents is royal or of high status; frequently it is the mother, while her husband may be a pathetic or minor figure. However, frequently it is not the husband but rather a god who impregnates the mother.
>
> *Conception.* The mother's pregnancy is often a mysterious or peculiar event, perhaps following years of barrenness or continence. In many myths she is a virgin.
>
> *Prophecy.* A dream or oracle forecasts that the coming boy will bring danger (especially to the husband) as well as greatness.
>
> *Abandonment.* Because of such a prophecy or for other reasons, the "father" sets the newborn out onto the water or in the wilderness to die.
>
> *Rescue and exile.* An animal or person of low status finds, hides, exchanges, or smuggles the infant to safety. He is reared in strange circumstances.
>
> *Return.* When grown, not knowing who he is, he embarks on a series of adventures or blind misadventures. At their end he finds himself in the city of his birth, where he kills or supplants his father.
>
> *Discovery.* His true identity is revealed, and he attains rank and honor.

As is apparent, the story of Oedipus fits Rank's model very well. Before going into psychological implications of these recurrent features of mythology, let us examine Raglan's (1949) model, which is broader in its cultural base:

(1) *The hero's mother is a royal virgin;*
(2) *His father is a king, and*
(3) *Often a near relative of his mother, but*
(4) *The circumstances of his conception are unusual, and*
(5) *He is also reputed to be the son of a god.*
(6) *At birth an attempt is made, usually by his father or his maternal grandfather, to kill him, but*
(7) *He is spirited away, and*
(8) *Reared by foster-parents in a far country.*
(9) *We are told nothing of his childhood, but*

(10) *On reaching manhood, he returns or goes to his future kingdom.*

(11) *After a victory over the king and/or a giant, dragon, or wild beast,*

(12) *He marries a princess, often the daughter of his predecessor, and*

(13) *Becomes king.* *

Again it is apparent that Oedipus fits the hero pattern quite well; *he is the most typical hero of those listed by Raglan.* ** Because it is also apparent that real-life heroes do not fit this pattern (i.e., their lives do not resemble those of the mythical hero, a point which Raglan develops at length), we have added reason to interpret the myth of the hero as a product of human fantasy.

Ideas of maternal virginity and unnatural conception and birth have remained meaningful in the Christian Era. Extraordinary conception plays a role in the supernatural status and powers associated with Jesus and Mary. *** The idea of a virginal mother and a nonsexual conception is fairly common in the fantasies of children and patients. Statements like, "She was disgusted by my father and flinched whenever he touched her. For years they slept in separate rooms. It's a miracle that I was ever born" are common in psychotherapy practice. The virginal image usually carries truth and fancy; it reflects a troubled relationship between a person's parents and it tends to exaggerate their sexual separation and specifically to deny the mother's sexuality. We may recognize in this distortion by a son an idealization of his mother (even if it is a crippling idealization), and a wish to separate her further from his father or to deny that his father has had her. Making mother virginal also emphasizes her hypothetical inaccessibility, thus helping a son to control his incestuous thoughts.

---

* Raglan followed the myth past the climax of the hero's life into his decline. After becoming king, "(14) For a time he reigns uneventfully, and (15) Prescribes laws, but (16) Later he loses favor with the gods and/or his subjects, and (17) Is driven from the throne and city, after which (18) He meets with a mysterious death, (19) Often at the top of a hill. (20) His children, if any, do not succeed him. (21) His body is not buried, but nevertheless (22) He has one or more holy sepulchres."

** Details bearing on points 18 to 22 are present in Sophocles' *Oedipus at Colonus* and in other versions of the Oedipus myth.

*** The same is true for Shakespeare's Macduff, who is also a savior. His peculiar birth, which makes him invulnerable, can be seen as a modern variation of the idea of heroes and supernatural creatures being conceived and born in atypical ways. Foundlings, changelings, and bastards were regarded with awe until recent times.

However the source of the idea of chastity in a mother has often been the mother herself. Many mothers have behaved like Victorian maidens in front of their children, giving the impression that the touch or kiss of a man repelled them. And they have fostered the idea of their virginity by fantastic explanations given to their children of how babies are born. Even though semiscientific explanations have replaced stories about storks, the roles of fathers are still often omitted or left vague. When this is so, the explanation given to a child that he grew from a seed in his mother's stomach still suggests immaculate conception.

The continued denial of maternal sexuality over so many centuries suggests a strong parental interest in the denial. We often hear parents say that children are not prepared for the full facts about reproduction. But it is evident that parents are not prepared to discuss their sexuality with their children. Some mothers say that fathers should explain reproduction and sex to sons because for mothers to do so would have sexual undertones. They are making explicit what is probably true for others as well. Mothers have been concerned about revealing their sexuality to their sons.

Raglan's third point, that the mother and father are close relatives, which is present in the Oedipus myth, introduces the theme of incest, suggesting that parents are capable of knowingly engaging in it. If, as in some of the myths, the mother has married her own father (or, by mating with a god, she is symbolically mating with her father), then father-daughter incest is clearly in the background. Thus the mother is the central figure in mythical incest, being involved in it before the hero's birth.

The theme of the father's attempt to kill the son may be viewed as a projection by a son of his own wish to kill his father. It could also serve as a rationalization for a son's wish (I will kill father because he is going to kill me). But what we know of ancient Mediterranean cultures suggests that the theme of killing the son represents a parental wish. Killing of newborn sons (and sometimes daughters) was practiced in a number of areas, including Greece. Infanticide often had sacrificial purposes and involved first-born children. In some cultures it was thought that a woman's husband was not necessarily the father of her first child;* therefore the father killed the first-born to protect

---

* In our culture, doubt about paternity is also more likely to focus on a first child, especially if he is born soon after the marriage. Raglan found that the hero was nearly always a first child.

the family's stability. In other words, a child of doubtful paternity was considered a threat. Here we have a cultural parallel and explanation for the first part of the myth: questionable paternity, mysterious conception, foreboding of danger, and the husband's attempt to kill the child.

In cases of doubtful paternity, the killing of the child was presumably more in the husband's interest than in the wife's. This was most true when it was felt that the son might become a rival to the father. A mother might share her husband's wish to destroy the child or she might not. In myth she often appeared as the infant's rescuer, hiding him (even hiding the fact that she had been pregnant and given birth), exchanging him, or spiriting him out of the country. Her secret support of the child against her husband and his interests can be interpreted as expressing a wish for the boy to supplant the husband. Such an interpretation best fits those myths in which the husband is portrayed as unworthy of her. Her intervention may also be seen as expressive of a boy's wish for his mother to take his side and prefer him over his father.

Killing of the father and mating with the mother are common themes in myth. When not portrayed specifically, they are usually suggested symbolically. That is, when the hero does not kill his father he kills an uncle (father's brother), king, aged man, giant, or dragon. Similarly, the hero may marry his sister or a king's widow or daughter rather than his own mother. The hero's parricide and incest have usually been interpreted as expressing a son's desire to eliminate his father and possess his mother. The obvious alternative, suggested above, is that these themes represent the wish of woman to be rid of an undesirable mate and find fulfillment with his successor. This interpretation is given additional weight later when community interests are considered in the shaping of myth.

An additional theme of the myth stressed by Rank (although omitted by Raglan) is the melodramatic prophecy, often revealed in a parent's dream, that precedes the hero's birth. As to prophecies revealed in dreams, we are on familiar ground in treating them as representing the fantasies of the dreamer (i.e., the parent). It was argued above that a prophecy revealed through an oracle may similarly be treated as a projection of the unconscious mind of the person consulting the oracle. A seer or an oracle, especially when he spoke in nonspecific or contradictory ways (for example, the Delphic Oracle's riddles, generalities, and symbols) served as a reflecting medium through which the client saw his own fantasies. In prophecy he saw them not as his own paltry wishes but as sacred destiny.*

We may assume that those who looked for omens in their dreams or consulted oracles, then as now, were those who particularly felt the need to—dissatisfied people. In the myth of Oedipus, desire for children was the motive of Laius and Jocasta in consulting the Oracle. Besdine (1969) has chosen the figure of Jocasta to represent modern women who, disappointed in their husbands, hunger for a son and lover. Jocasta of the myth is a talented, passionate woman. Her unhappy marriage and barren life are due entirely to deficiencies in her husband. As scholars of Greek drama have remarked, not a single redeeming feature has been given to Laius in the story. He is ineffectual, superstitious, easily frightened, and ready to disrupt and destroy lives in order to allay his fears. Unmanly, afraid to father children, afraid to be a lover to his wife, he offers her no possibilities for happiness. In addition, the image of a husband who is unworthy and is disposed of, the situation of a wife whose creativity and love have been suppressed and whose situation appears hopeless, and the advent of a virile prince who rescues the woman—these themes suggest a woman's viewpoint.** Oedipus, the young prince, is the fulfillment of Jocasta's dream. He is brilliant and manly; the feats he performs bring hope to her. And he liberates her. In the flowering of her love for her son she comes alive. The Delphic Oracle's prophecy—the coming of a son who will kill the father and be a lover to the mother—represents the fulfillment of Jocasta's needs, not Laius'. (And it is Laius, not Jocasta, who tries to prevent the prophecy from coming true.) *Thus the prophecy that is the keynote of the myth of Oedipus represents a woman's fantasy.*

The idea that Greek myths represent the wishes of oppressed women for vindication, revenge, liberation, and consummation of frustrated sexuality was suggested by Deutsch (1969). In myths about Dionysus, a chief object of worship in ancient Greece, she saw the hero's mission as liberation of women. His mission derived from the humiliation and injury suffered by his mother. Such an interpretation

---

* It would seem likely that the ancient seer, who often sold his oracles like today's "adviser," was skilled in telling the client what he (secretly) wanted to hear. Fenichel (1945) suggested that the ambiguity of the oracle corresponded to the contradictory wishes of the client. Destiny (Fate) is female.

** The need of the plague-ridden land of Thebes for a savior coincides with Jocasta's needs. Later in the chapter we will see other ways in which mother and country (earth) have equivalent meanings in hero myth.

fits the situation of middle- and upper-class women in that culture.*
Disenfranchised politically and neglected by their husbands, they
turned to their sons. The typical family of ancient Greece—a frustrated mother restricted to the home and dominant in it, a father
occupied elsewhere, and a son with Oedipal problems—resembles the
family of the mythical hero. It also seems to be the typical family of
today's hero (see below).**

THE RITES OF SPRING

Jocasta, like women of Athens, was bound by cultural patterns.
She could not free herself from the hopeless condition that resulted
from her marriage. Therefore she needed someone to do it for her.
Similarly, Thebes, like other dispirited communities, looked to a
champion for salvation. Oedipus fitted the needs of the woman and
the city because he was alienated; lack of purpose and confusion about
his identity made him available to enlist in the causes of others. *Alienation, thus, is more than a common feature of heroes; it is a prerequisite.*
The necessity for their alienation becomes clearer when we explore the
origins of hero myths. In tracing myth to ritual beginnings and in
tracing the hero to his ancestor, the priest-king, Raglan's (1949) and
Frazer's (1940) reconstructions of data from pre-classic Greece and
other ancient cultures will be followed. In some cultures referred to,
the relevant practices persisted until recent times, even into this century.***

---

* Slater (1971) suggested that mother-son relationships determined the content
of Greek hero-god myths.

** The chapter began with the idea of women who feel oppressed and deprived
and therefore look for a hero. We are especially concerned with women who do not
get sexual satisfaction from their husbands or from anyone else, women whose
career ambitions and creative talents have been put aside for marriage or stifled
by their husbands. By tradition such women have been socially limited to one outlet—having children. Until recently few of them fought these limitations; the
majority submitted to their fates. Victorian culture presented an extreme of civilization in this respect. The Victorian woman who adopted her prescribed role was
not only frigid, she was languid, like the earth in winter. She and most of her
daughters up to the present were not prepared to free themselves.

*** Even though we recognize features of the hero myth in the stories of Moses
and Jesus, the hero myth as well as the religious practices described below may
seem remote from modern Western religion and culture. However some Jewish
and Christian concepts of man, embedded in the Bible, define him as alienated. The
story of Creation makes man an outcast from paradise, seeking reentry. Born out of
his mother's anguish and bearing the sin of Adam, he has many labors to perform
before full acceptance is accorded him. In addition, he is born as a child, and by

Frazer, in *The Golden Bough,* described an unusual custom in which men lived in isolated huts or caves, sometimes in chains. Known as kings, they were the titular rulers of their communities. However their functions were priestly rather than administrative. They were engaged in propitiating gods for the benefit of their subjects; ritual was their main activity. In some cultures priest-kings exercised civil as well as priestly powers, but shared with these isolates the melodrama of the beginning and end of their term of office. The way they were removed from office as well as the ritual by which they lived marked them as ceremonial figures who possessed little personal identity.

In some cultures a priest-king's term depended on his "success"; for example, when the crops failed, his subjects deposed or killed him. Along the Nile his term depended on his retention of youthful vigor, with death when he fell ill, showed signs of aging, or failed to satisfy his many wives sexually (and it was their duty to report his failure). In most cultures reported, his term was fixed, ranging from one day in the Congo, with one year in Babylonia and Mexico as well as Greece, to twelve years in India; at the end of his term he was killed.

In some Greek cities the spring fertility festival seems to have marked the end of the old king's reign and life, and the accession of the new one, including his marriage to the newly widowed queen.* Here, where the office was actively sought, trials were established to choose a suitable successor, including feats of physical ability. (Raglan speculated that these contests developed into the Greek games later known as the Olympics.)

However the office was not always sought. In Cambodia and West Africa, candidates resisted violently and greatness had to be thrust upon them. And in Sierra Leone, deliberate malice played a part in the election of the king. A more serious political consequence occurred in Niue where, after a long period of killing kings when the crops were poor, no one would serve and the monarchy ended.

A trend that was more conserving of kings as well as monarchies involved the use of substitution and symbolism. The king resigned or was symbolically killed, and he hid while his successor reigned for

---

traditional views this makes him a creature without reason, governed by instinct or emotion. Only by a series of initiations can he become a man. He has a long way to go to find his place and his human identity. As Fromm (1955) pointed out, in the Biblical tradition he has to leave home and wander among strangers in order to find himself.

* These practices suggest the origin of those myths in which the youth (Oedipus) kills the old king or tyrant and marries his widow (Jocasta).

a week, copulating with the "widow" and serving as a reincarnation of the old king. At the end of these rites, the substitute was killed or deposed and the old king returned, rejuvenated in the process.

Reference to sex in these replacement or rejuvenation procedures is not incidental. Belief that priest-kings could and did "fertilise the earth and confer other benefits on their subjects would seem to have been shared by the ancestors of all the Aryan races from India to Ireland. . . ." (Frazer, 1940). And their power to fertilize the earth was seen as connected to their power to fertilize women. People believed in a close connection between ritual act and practical application. A king who was not prepared to demonstrate sexual power was considered a handicap to his community.*

The fertility of the fields, as a reality and as a symbol of productivity and well-being generally, was what was vital to the community. For these reasons, spring rites (which were fertility rites) were marked by sexual orgies engaged in by the king, his queen, and the specially selected youths who substituted for them. Although pleasure later motivated increasingly large numbers of the populace to join in the festivities (for example, in Europe in the Middle Ages and even in this century in Germany), their participation retained vestiges of a ceremonial function.

By extension of simple analogical reasoning and by symbolic elaboration, more and more of the priest-king's behavior came to be considered critical to his subjects' welfare, and he became increasingly ruled by taboos. For example, kings were forbidden to copulate, to touch the earth, to cut their hair or nails, or even to walk, except when these things were done ceremonially, which meant on a schedule and in a prescribed manner. Besides the king, his heir (when known ahead of time, as by birth in later cultures) was subject to constraints upon his eating, drinking, posture, locomotion, bathing, dressing, and sex. Irish kings observed taboos as to path and direction when traveling, and were even restricted as to position of head and body when sleeping. The chief priest of Rome, for whom every day was considered holy and therefore circumscribed, was forbidden to say common words like goat, dog, raw meat, and ivy. Associated with this ritualization of behavior were beliefs of awesome consequences resulting

---

* By similar reasoning, farmers were unhappy with barren wives, not so much because they wanted heirs as because they feared that the fields would become or remain barren until the women were disposed of. The practice of farmers divorcing barren wives has persisted into recent times (Levy-Bruhl, 1924).

from violation of the taboos. In the extreme it was believed that if the priest-king moved or touched something or was touched by some thing or person, except as prescribed, destruction of the world would follow. For these reasons, Frazer (1940) said,

> . . . *people will exact of their king or priest a strict conformity to those rules, the observance of which is deemed necessary for his own preservation, and consequently for the preservation of his people and the world. The idea that early kingdoms are des-potisms in which people exist only for the sovereign, is wholly inapplicable to the monarchies we are considering. On the con-trary, the sovereign in them exists only for his subjects. . . .*

Thus the life of the king tended to become increasingly artificial, as did the lives of those who aspired or were chosen to become king and prepared themselves accordingly. *Such a person could not do many things spontaneously, naturally or in consequence of his own instincts or emotions.* For him to have or be aware of desires or aver-sions in connection with activities that were governed by taboo would not only be irrelevant but could interfere with the proper performance of his job or even endanger the world. It would seem likely that train-ing to become king meant training in the suppression of impulses and feelings and in the suppression of a sense of personal identity. Where there were many taboos, Frazer found that priest-kings sank under the weight of office into "spiritless creatures, cloistered recluses," into apathy and weakness which enabled ambitious men to rule them as puppets from behind the scenes. Others became fanatics and thus were less obviously alienated. But they were alienated from people and society, and mostly from their own feelings and thoughts—from their selves.

A king whose faith was strong enjoyed the illusion of supreme power, of being himself divine or embodying the power of a god. He could believe that a tiny movement of his finger could cause destruc-tion. But he also knew that he was not free to do things that were not prescribed. All of his acts had great religious and political meaning, but no personal meaning because he performed them as a ceremonial figure. He personified the society, but was not a member of it; no one was more remote and cut off from the life of the community than he. He stood for the greatest of gods, but was hardly a man, for he lacked feelings, impulses, and personal identity. Often he lacked even an individual name, bearing only that of the dead hero or god whom he incarnated.

Candidates for the office were not related by blood to the king and queen and in some cultures convention required that they be strangers to the community. Thus neither incest nor parricide were involved at this stage of civilization.* But as time brought the institution of hereditary kings we may infer that, in the grafting of new traditions onto old, royal mating tended toward incest and regicide toward parricide in some cultures. A fusing of old and new patterns is found in many myths in which, like Oedipus, the conquering hero is simultaneously a stranger and the hereditary successor.

It has been suggested that hero myths are projections of personal needs of people, especially mothers. Combining communal origins of hero myths with personal interests that perpetuate them, it would seem that the common hero myth is an expression of the wishes of people who feel oppressed and dispirited. Below and in later chapters, alienation in students, psychopaths, and gamblers will be interpreted as an outgrowth of the demand for heroes and scapegoats by people who seek inspiration and redemption.

If the hero myth represents a merger of the interests of communities and of women, those interests must be similar, at least symbolically. Raglan (1949) stressed agricultural needs of communities as basic to the origin of the office of the priest-king and to his becoming a key actor in the spring rites. The hero myth, by its recitation in connection with spring rites, had the function of restoring the cold, dead earth to a fertile condition. Mother and earth have long been equated symbolically. The priest-king's ceremonial intercourse with the royal mother or vestal substitute was specifically intended to make the earth fertile. Therefore we may infer that the hero, by rescuing and mating with special women in the myth, was symbolically rescuing and fertilizing the land.

Putting the above practices and beliefs together, it is possible to suggest a line of development producing the alienated hero of mythology and classical tragedy. Raglan's (1949) view of the beginning is that in difficult circumstances people turned for help to those who had a propensity for ritual magic and elevated them to positions of responsibility. Thus the first king of the line might have been a rainmaker.

---

* Symbolically, incest was involved. The successor became by initiation the son of his predecessor and thus of the widow, whom he married.

Besides controlling weather, he was typically expected to promote fertility in women and animals, success in hunting, fishing, and war, and freedom from disease. Nowhere, to begin with, was morality relevant to the performance of his function. A good king was one whose subjects fared well, exactly as a good rainmaker was one who made rain. "The ideal is one, not of supreme moral perfection, but of supreme functional efficiency." But piety soon became a prerequisite of kingship because of the common belief that natural forces were regulated by gods, often specifically by that god who was the established patron or founding father of the community. Therefore a good priest-king would be one who had good standing with the god and could intercede with him.

Communion with spirits or gods might most fittingly be done in seclusion, but we are not dealing here with genuine functional efficiency. Rather than rainmaking, we are concerned with the appearance of rainmaking, and similarly the appearance of divine communion. The ancient priest-king had to impress people with his potency in order to justify and retain his position. Because he could not actually control the elements, the performance of impressive public feats was called for. These had the primary function of impressing an audience, inspiring the faithful, renewing their morale, especially during a period of hardship (drought, plague). In this respect the hermit king was atypical; the more usual practice involved very public rites, and in some places popular attendance was compulsory.

In Greece the main rites developed into an annual spectacular involving athletics, dramatics, and the sacrifice of the reigning king plus the initiation and wedding of the new one. These and similar spring rites in other cultures have been widely interpreted as a morale-building renewal of spirit and activity after the decay and despair of winter, and morale building would seem to have become the primary function of the main or spectacular Greek rites. Eliade (1965) interpreted initiatory rites generally as consisting of a reenactment of the story of creation, and thereby constituting a revival of god, nature, or whatever vital force has become dormant. Eliade, Frazer, and Raglan stressed the retelling of the story of creation—which is also the story of the life of the primal hero, the creator or founder of the community—as part of the rites. And this ritual narration was seen as developing into the heroic tragedy performed as part of the rites during the flowering of Greek drama. If the ritual narration served as part of the initiation of the new priest-king, we may infer that its content was an allegory of his life and role woven around elements from the myth of the patron god. The alienation, dedication, and sacrifice of the hero of classic drama probably carried over from those themes in the ritual narration.*

THE DISMEMBERED KING

"Everyone knows that the performance of Greek tragedy in the fifth century B.C. was part of a religious ritual in honor of Dionysus and that the plots of Greek tragedy are nearly all drawn from myth," said Kirkwood (1958). Fergusson (1949) called *Oedipus Rex* a passion play and stressed its inspirational function:

> *The figure of Oedipus himself fulfills all the requirements of the scapegoat, the dismembered king or god-figure. The situation in which Thebes is presented at the beginning of the play—in peril of its life; its crops, its herd, its women mysteriously infertile, signs of a mortal disease of the City, and the disfavor of the gods—is like the withering which winter brings, and calls, in the same way, for struggle, dismemberment, death, and renewal. And this tragic sequence is the substance of the play.*

The practice of exploiting the priest-king during his term of office and then killing him suggests the source for the ending of the typical myth, in which the hero is cast out after performing his function (Raglan, 1949).** The scapegoating of the hero is not made explicit in many myths, but is in *Oedipus Rex*.

Scapegoating was obvious in those cultures where the king was killed when his people were frustrated, as by poor crops. The practice elsewhere of putting him to death at the end of a fixed term may seem

---

* In connecting heroes of myth and drama to priest-kings and founding gods, I stressed masculine power in relation to community welfare and particularly fertility. Although founders of communities were typically male, many cultures worshipped earth goddesses or other females as controlling the crops or the hunt. Therefore the central place given here to the community-service function of the hero does not imply that the communities involved primarily worshipped male gods. The role of hero was adaptable to mother worship as well as father worship. Where worship of an earth goddess prevailed, the hero (like his forebear, the priest-king) seems to have served as the main intermediary between her and the community.

** The mystery of his death suggests a sacrament, and, in myth, Oedipus became a god and protector of Athens at his death.

more humane, but it was only a more orderly practice. It was no less exploitative. Either way the king was treated as an instrument for the satisfaction of his people. Whether or not his killing was done as part of a periodic religious rite, his life and the taking of it bore little connection to him as an individual, but reflected the needs of others. The purest example of rendering a person into nothing more than an object was the practice among Phoenicians of killing the first male child at birth. Whether one is killed on being born or on attaining manhood makes no basic difference here; either way he is treated essentially as an object or instrument.

Returning to Oedipus, we see that he is an excellent example of the exploited hero. Little that he does in Thebes is for personal gain. In killing his father he unwittingly relieves the community of an aged, sexually inadequate king, one who has not met its needs. In destroying the Sphinx, marrying his mother, assuming the throne, and in answering the question of who killed his father, he serves the community's needs rather than his own. In Sophocles' portrait, Oedipus' irritability, arrogance, suspiciousness, and quickness to destroy others and himself do not detract from the fact that he does little to further his own needs or desires and that he does not initiate things but rather responds to others' demands. Twice he saves the community, risking his life in the process. He comes to the Thebans as a lost wanderer, and having served their needs, he departs more an outcast than before. That he is deified in the end makes him no less exploited and alienated.

To say that Oedipus is a hero is not to say that he is a virtuous person. A savior, he is also an agent of corruption; he destroys and redeems, often at the same time. This duality is basic to his character; many times during the play his hesitation between dedicated service and destructive fury heightens the suspense. The duality also seems basic to his role. The priest-king was always a party to killing in the very act that rejuvenated his land and people. Destroying and becoming were joined together. Eliade (1965) argued that death and dismemberment, at least symbolically, are part of every significant initiatory rite because initiation means transfiguration, rebirth as a new, different person with a new identity. He stressed the primitive belief that death is a prerequisite for change. Whether or not these are universal beliefs, it does seem that the priest-kings generally placed little value on living (although paradoxically their mission was to foster life); they willingly killed and let themselves be killed. The "king for a day" was the extreme example, committing suicide in effect on the very day that he was reborn. But the heroes we have considered were all indirectly suicidal as well as homicidal. Oedipus' recklessness, inviting death in his encounters, is not atypical. When he confronted his father with an escort, they were several to his one, and when he confronted the Sphinx, the odds against him were much greater. In these encounters and when he blinded himself there was no indication that he felt that he had anything of substance to lose. (Suicidal behavior will be discussed as an important feature of alienated people in Chapter 4.)

Norman (1969) suggested that the essence of the mythical hero is total risk and dedication. And Slochower (1961) argued that the mythical hero is necessarily destructive and criminal, that his character or role pits him as a youth against the established rules. He steals, commits incest and parricide, and as a consequence is exiled. Slochower felt that the hero's crime and his challenge to authority are the very deeds that redeem and transform his rotten, dying community. Thus destruction and redemption would seem closely connected.

In emphasizing the exploitation of the hero, no implication that he was coerced into his role is intended. Many priest-kings and other heroes were willing enough victims. The hero-to-be has the option of refusal, of rejecting the pleas of the city for redemption and of the temptress for a mate, and instead following his own personal interests. But it would seem that in reaching the point in life where these demands are placed upon him he has gone too far to be able to turn away without paying a heavy price. The possibilities for having a personal, selfish life have been much narrowed in his character development, as Campbell (1956) points out:

> *Often in actual life, and not infrequently in the myths and popular tales, we encounter the dull case of the call unanswered. . . . Refusal of the summons converts the adventure into its negative. Walled in boredom, hard work or "culture," the subject loses the power of significant affirmative action and becomes a victim to be saved. His flowering world becomes a wasteland of dry stones and his life meaningless—even though . . . he may through titanic effort succeed in building an empire of renown. Whatever house he builds, it will be a house of death. . . . All he can do is create new problems for himself and wait the gradual approach of his disintegration.*

JOCASTA MOTHERING

The hero-to-be, the one who accepts the invitation, challenge, or mission, may expect to find beyond the barriers a special woman. In Campbell's (1956) interpretation she is the ultimate woman, "the Queen Goddess of the World . . . the paragon of all paragons. . . . She is the mother, sister, mistress, bride." She is both a stranger and one whom he knew in his remote past and remains youthfully preserved in the images that inspire his search. Sometimes she is pictured as sleeping. His coming awakens her for a triumphant union.

She is a representation of mother nature at the end of winter: barren but ready to spring to life; ancient and yet capable of radiant beauty. She is the one who gave him life, and to whom he will give life, the one whom he first tasted and who will forever exemplify the meaning of a special woman, different or divine. Campbell notes that she is also the "bad" mother: absent, unattainable, forbidden, punitive, "whose presence is a lure to dangerous desire. . . ."

A popular representation of this young-old woman is the heroine of *Sleeping Beauty*. Like a severely depressed person she lies in her bed in a deathlike torpor, waiting for a young prince to bring her to life. She is not a nymph to be taken lightly; she lures men to death. But her revival by the hero brings life to her community. Although dormant and helpless in the sense of being unable to free herself, her influence is powerful.

In myth Jocasta is a woman of fifty who has remained untouched sexually most of her life. Her husband had avoided her for years before she became pregnant and again afterward during the time in which Oedipus grew to manhood. In Sophocles' portrait she appears as a reckless temptress. Divine injunctions, solemn warnings and the traditional values with which she has lived are brushed aside as in the late bloom of her love she defies male authority so that she can have her young prince.* She is a desperate woman; her passion has been denied an outlet and she is growing old. The arrival of her son awakens her to the crowning love of her life. It also sets in motion a chain of events from which he emerges as an outcast.

This Jocasta is not only a legend of her time and a prototype of

---

* Interpreters of drama have commented on Jocasta's inordinate love, disregard of codes and consequences, and the pressure she exerts on her hesitant son toward extreme acts (Ehrenberg, 1968). See also O'Brien (1968) and Kirkwood (1958) on her impulsiveness and irresponsibility.

women who are unfulfilled and yearn for children; she has been re-discovered in the modern mother. Although only rarely does sexual intercourse actually occur between mother and son, the frustrated woman, seething with half-hidden feelings and desires which she focuses on one of her children, has been repeatedly identified in the last two decades as the mother of disturbed sons, alienated youth, and even Americans generally. Troubled men of our time are pictured increasingly in psychological literature as coming from families that sound typically American. The father is apt to be a background figure; he may be highly successful in his career, but he spends little time at home or is passive, inept, or detached when there. The mother dom-inates the household; having aborted her career and been disappointed in her husband, she focuses her talents, energy, and fantasies on a son. This son, insofar as he devotes himself to fulfilling his mother and her fantasies, seems to develop without a clear sense of himself. A few lines of research on this mother-son combination will be considered.

Besdine (1968) suggested that such chosen sons grow up to be extraordinarily egocentric and masochistic. They pursue unattainable women and life goals, missing or avoiding the intimacy for which they yearn. They become geniuses, homosexuals, and addicts. Many of them seem so compulsive and unemotional as to give the impression of dehumanized creatures.

The Jocasta mother is typically a bright, warm, forceful woman, although these qualities are often hidden. Her gifts of intellect and love are not available to her husband nor to other men. She may appear cold to the world. But with a favorite son she establishes "a close, binding, intimate, and exclusive lover's relationship, making him her chief love object. . . ." (Besdine, 1970).

This intense attachment results from her sexual frustration and craving for children, according to Besdine (1968). The cause of her deprivation may be an absent, distant, or aged husband, delayed mar-riage, severe conflict between husband and wife, failure to conceive, and miscarriage or loss of a child. Modern social conditions that sharpen women's frustration are also relevant.

Frustrated and depressed, the mother responds to her infant with what Besdine called "Jocasta mothering." She seeks solace for herself in his love, drawing him to her in despair and misery. She overevalu-ates the boy and overprotects and indulges him, but also is seductive and narcissistic with him, dominating his emotions and making heavy demands of him. But she does not do these things consistently; frightened of her attachment and dependence (for she has been badly disappointed before), and shocked by her sensual feelings for the boy and by his arousal in response to her, she also pushes him away.

The effect of the irregular rebuffs is to provoke the boy to greater effort. He seeks constantly to exceed himself: he trains and tries again, harder and harder, to win her tenderness, to win back the paradise she is denying him. A number of courses are open to him. He may go on to higher and higher achievement, becoming a creative genius or a superstar. He may become erratic, starting one ambitious scheme after another only to abandon them. Or he may give up the struggle to a larger extent, withdrawing, perhaps with the help of alcohol or drugs, or finding a substitute striving like gambling.

Typically Oedipus is an only son. When a severely frustrated woman has more than one child she may look to all of them for fulfillment. But her demands produce the most dramatic effects when she singles out one child as her champion. Besdine (1969) suggested that her choice is likely to fall on her first-born, or her first to survive after the loss of a child. Also likely is a child born late, after other children have grown and gone. My own impression is that a child born after the death of the mother's father or another close relative is often chosen, or one born when his parents are particularly unhappy with each other. Also relevant are any number of circumstances that cause loneliness and a sense of desperation in a depression-prone woman.

The widely held idea that alienation is on the increase in America was discussed in the last chapter. Besdine and Slater see more Jocasta mothering, more fostering of Oedipal children as an outgrowth of our culture, which is becoming increasingly child-centered in harmful ways. The following is Slater's (1970) analysis.

The ambition of our middle-class parents is to bear super-children. This is especially true of suburban mothers who are sexually distant from their husbands and socially isolated in the home with little to do except to devote themselves to children:

> . . . when the parent turns to the child as a vicarious substitute for satisfactions the parent fails to find in his or her own life . . . the child becomes vain, ambitious, hungry for glory. Both the likelihood and the intensity of this pattern are increased when the family is a small, nuclear, isolated unit and the child socialized by few other adults. Our society has from the beginning, and increasingly with each generation, tended to foster "Oedipal children."

Comparing a variety of societies, those

> . . . in which deprived mothers turn to their children for what
> they cannot obtain from adults tend to produce males who are
> vain, boastful, aggressive, and skittish toward women. Such males
> have great fear of losing self-control, of becoming dependent upon
> women, of weakness.

Mothers deprived of sex with men are especially likely to be seductive, consciously or unconsciously, with their sons, and the significance of their seductiveness depends on family structure. In families
where a mother is one of many women with whom a boy has contact
daily, her seductiveness has limited effects. But where she is the only
woman and is with him all the time in his first years, her son is likely
to become extremely disturbed, according to Slater. In our culture,
with the decline of the extended family and the resultant limited
contact that little boys have with other women, the effects of Jocasta
mothers on their sons become increasingly serious.

Slater (1971) compared our culture to Athens of the Classical
Period, where similar conditions appeared in starker form. There he
found the situation of middle- and upper-class women to be extremely
frustrating. Although cultured, wives were more segregated, helpless,
and dependent on their husbands than they are today. And Athenian
husbands, strangers to their homes and contemptuous of their wives,
neglected them badly. Homosexually oriented, husbands preferred men
generally and as lovers over their women. Even many who were heterosexual preferred courtesans to the low-status creatures at home.

Excluded from the social and political life of the community, and
hating their husbands, the women turned to their sons.* The sons
received inordinate love and attention from their mothers, whose fantasies they were expected to fulfill. The position of these sons was

---

* Slater found particularly intense mother-son relationships in cultures in which
sex antagonism was high and women's status low and their envy of men high. To
say that our culture is extreme in producing Oedipal sons does not mean that
women's status is extremely low now. On the contrary, women were more oppressed in pre-Victorian times. However, women were conditioned to expect much
less in the past and were probably less frustrated sexually. It is the combination of
education, ambition, and expectation of fulfillment with oppression, isolation,
and exclusive power over children that our suburban women share with their
Athenian counterparts. Intense antagonism toward men is unlikely to be found in
women who are abject slaves. Pride in self and contempt for the oppressor would
seem to be necessary for the kind of mothering described here as well as for a
revolution of rising expectations.

complicated by their mothers' hostility toward men, which manifested itself in intolerance of masculine traits in the sons. Thus the sons' task was nearly impossible: to be lovers and heroes while being punished for signs of masculinity. The result was that sons turned away from their mothers, growing hostile to women as they grew up. When they married, they treated their wives badly. Thus the cycle was self-perpetuating.

The main effect on the son of an intense mother-son relationship is narcissism, according to Slater. He distinguished four forms of it: high achievement drive, unscrupulousness (psychopathic character), homosexuality, and schizophrenia. The first three seem to have been common in Athens of that time, with ambition and unscrupulousness combined in the drive to be heroes. When they could not be heroic, Athenian men felt that they were nothing. Their sense of self was thus grandiose but fragile, requiring the greatest effort to uphold. Pride and prestige were everything to them; they were highly self-conscious, abnormally concerned about how others viewed them, and oversensitive to slights. Yet they constantly made themselves vulnerable by their competitiveness and recklessness.

Recklessness was not merely incidental to their determination to be heroes; it was an ingredient of heroism. They lived as gamblers. Slater noted the "willingness, even the compulsion, to risk everything, including one's life, for fame and glory. . . ." The Athenians undertook an invasion of Sicily even though Athens was under siege by Sparta at the time; "the very foolhardiness of the adventure . . . made it so appealing. . . . The more its hazards were stressed, the more they favored it."

As figures, they were inspiring by virtue of their intelligence and creativity as well as their heroism. But as people, Slater thought them very difficult to get along with. In Thucydides' description,*

> . . . they are adventurous beyond their power and daring beyond their judgment. . . . Thus they toil on in trouble and danger all the days of their life, with little opportunity for enjoying. . . . To describe their character in a word, one might truly say that they were born into the world to take no rest themselves and to give none to others.

---

* Quoted in Slater (1971). If we allow for exaggeration in this picture of Athenian character it comes closer to American character.

Many of today's radical youth seem to resemble Athenians in character and in their relationships with their mothers. Keniston (1968), in his in-depth study of militant students, gave the following picture of their childhoods. Their mothers were very close to them and heavily invested in them, with extreme attachments developing in the first years of life. From the beginning the sons felt that they were special and submitted willingly to their fates, showing unusual responsiveness to their mothers' wishes, especially in academic achievement. They performed. They were good athletes, presidents of their classes, and later were outstanding college students.

However their good fortune was not without its price; their adolescent years were marked by severe inner turmoil and suffering. They approached manhood with intense feelings of weakness, loneliness and sinfulness, and were especially troubled about sex.

But it was not their own problems which engaged their greatest energies; rather, they devoted themselves to causes, to alleviating the suffering of others. Thus, in becoming protesters and revolutionaries, their roles as champions for others were consistent with their childhood orientation of bringing fulfillment to their mothers.

These highly committed radicals had in common with mythical heroes parentage of unusually high status. And the same was true for a different group studied by Keniston (1965), which he called "the uncommitted." The two groups of collegians had similar beginnings and early records of extraordinary achievement. The radicals, continuing on to heroic, redemptive activities, may be thought of as those who answered the call. The uncommitted were those who refused it. They were college students who were extremely detached from their situation. Classes, job goals, and socializing meant little to them. Some persevered with studies and daily activities which had become a dreary routine. Others no longer maintained even the appearance of involvement; dropping out of classes without making alternate plans, they retained only tenuous connections with their college. Among the elite parents of this disengaged group, again it was the mothers who stood out, appearing to their sons as "vivid, sensuous and magnetic . . . talented, artistic, intense, and intelligent girls who gave up promise and fulfillment for marriage" (Keniston, 1968). But marriage brought them disappointment. While attaching themselves to their sons, these mothers excluded their husbands from the emotional life of the family. They openly disparaged their husbands, who apparently responded with bitter detachment from the family. The husbands turned more and more to outside interests, leaving their wives and sons "locked in a special alliance."

As seen through the eyes of the alienated sons, these family situations were Oedipal. The typical home was dominated by a talented, passionate woman who considered her husband unworthy of her and turned for satisfaction to her son. The husband, while not literally disposed of, had been largely displaced, and the son became an outstanding performer. Understandably, the half-conscious fantasies of the sons reflected the Oedipal family triangles they had perceived as children. On projective psychological tests there were two main themes in the fantasies they produced. One was an image of paradise lost together with a search for reunification with a long-lost lover. The other theme was of a "Pyrrhic Oedipal Victory," in which a triangle was resolved by a youth killing his father or elder and then being overcome by disaster. Thus the fantasies of these students resembled traditional hero myths.

The detached and the dropouts in Keniston's study remind us of many students today. Education, work, and life seem pointless to them, and they lack the resources to change their situation to a more meaningful one. The more extreme among them, estranged from themselves, from others, and from society, seem to be drifting in utter hopelessness, like those described by Campbell as having refused the call. Follow-up data on them are lacking. Probably some of them contribute to the exceptionally high suicide rate among college students. Many leave college, giving up earlier goals eventually to struggle for a more meaningful life. And many others pull themselves together long enough to graduate and continue into careers that are spiritually moribund for them.

□ 3. THE HIGH ROAD

When Gary Shaw graduated from high school, fifteen colleges offered him scholarships. With a mixture of awe and eagerness, he chose one high in prestige. On the campus he was a member of the football elite, enjoying the privileges and performing the labors that set him above other students. However, within four years, he was a confused, depressed wanderer, going from one odd job to another, searching for direction. His story (as told later in the chapter) highlights alienating processes along the road to greatness in college.

The career of the high performer who becomes a dropout begins at home. His first call comes from one or both parents early in childhood. By the time he enters school, he is already a performer and pleaser. Understandably, teachers are attracted to such a child. They see him as showing promise; they encourage him further, giving him privileges and responsibilities.* By high school he is recognized as a candidate and is guided into a college preparatory program. His teachers have begun to fit him for the special possibilities that lie ahead even though he has only the vaguest notions of his future. The oppor-

---

* This idealized, overly simple sequence does not fit those who are erratic, withdrawn, or rebellious in their early years and may not be recognized as promising until later.

tunities offered him and the price he will pay in pursuing them become clearer in college, where, perhaps for the first time, he may consider that he has a choice, that he can turn away.

Schools are society's main instrument for making its needs known to youth. Schools prepare youth to receive the call and select those who will hear it. And when the call becomes clear, many students do what they have been preparing for all their lives—they answer it. Others surprise and upset parents and school officials by refusing. (Probably the severity of our disappointment, reflecting the loftiness of our expectations, contributes to the resentment and even contempt with which we speak of dropouts.) Still others pass through without being called. They, the majority, participate in only a remote way in the drama of selection and initiation, and are less affected by it. In discussing academic and other experiences which bring a candidate to the point of accepting or refusing the call, two examples will be used. One is a boy chosen for academic excellence; the other, a high school football star.

The hero of mythology was a stranger wherever he went because he had been separated from his heritage. A group that particularly suffers from such separation is blacks. In general children of immigrants, of the poor, and of "minorities" have been pulled away from their already tenuous roots by our schools. For these groups the tension between the culture of the home and school, between parent and teacher, has long been recognized. That tension has been greatest for bright children, the ones whom teachers found most attractive and whom society most wanted.

The situation of exceptional black boys in our schools has been a striking example of culturally promoted alienation. Such children, because of the promise seen in them, have been given special privileges, opportunities, and initiations. Their experiences will be used here not primarily to describe the condition of blacks but to highlight alienating aspects of leadership induction. The situations which exceptional black boys encounter are fundamentally American, deriving from institutions that shape the character of white youth as well as black. Children who are not exceptional also have maturational experiences like those of the boy described below, but not to the same extent.

The boy who is our example, taken from Ellison's (1953) sociological novel, is graduating from high school, on the verge of manhood, about to embark on a search for his place in the world. The setting is a black high school in a Southern town a few decades ago. Times have changed and people from some parts of the country will find the folk-ways unfamiliar. However the practices described form a bridge be-tween the primitive rites described in the last chapter and more fa-miliar aspects of our culture.

THE STAGE

The boy we will follow has been chosen to deliver the valedictory oration. As he prepares his speech, we may consider his mental state and the nature of the task he confronts. The farewell speech is tradi-tionally as well as logically a prelude to the future, to life as an adult. As such, it is a speech about a world that has been presented to chil-dren as a conglomerate of ideals and illusions (often romanticized sweetly) and of realities (sometimes harsh). The task of the valedic-torian is to speak about and make sense of a mixture of the Ten Commandments and the business rat race, of the Protestant Ethic and the ruthless opportunism of the Western pioneer. Every valedictorian (and, to a lesser extent, every graduate) is thus called on to make sense of serious contradictions in our culture. What sense will this one arrive at? He is a boy with ideas; will he use them? How bold will he be? We can imagine some of his conflicts as he works on his speech. We can also predict what he, as a member of the sociological class of valedic-torians, will say and how he will say it.

To begin with, the fact that he has been chosen by his school to give the speech tells us that he has been a boy who pleased his teachers, behaved himself, and achieved success in the public school system. He has been chosen by one of the most conventional of our institutions, known for the pettiness of its rules. He has shown mastery of the well-worn paths that are open to our students. He simply cannot have been anti-establishment. As valedictorian he is called upon to inspire and to lead his fellow graduates, to furnish them with some vision and justification of their future. His role, on this day, is that of leader. Until now he has conformed to the system and done it well. He has been nurtured and rewarded by it, and today he stands publicly spon-sored by it as it calls upon him to lead his fellows. What will he do?

The traditional solution has been boldness of rhetoric combined with conventionality of content. Generations of valedictorians have used fiery words, imaginative images, and brilliant logic, and used them to praise the system. The general pattern is clearly established for the valedictorian, as well as the style to be used. He will put intense feeling into his speech. He knows the audience will expect ringing sincerity, and he is probably keyed up by the occasion. His past and future come together in this moment as he stands on the auditorium stage, aware of doors even if he cannot read the signs on them. The situation calls for him to be very serious, to suppress some of his impulses and ideas (including the half-realized one that the system is his enemy) and to suppress his reservations about the conventional message he will deliver. If he follows tradition, he will speak with a swelling voice and the exaggerated emotional emphasis of the announcer or public speaker. He may even convince himself of his sincerity.

Thus his speech will be an alienating experience. The style may be partly his own, and the verbal images his own, but the content is transmitted through him. He becomes, on this occasion, a clever, stylized mouthpiece.*

Having given the expected speech at the school auditorium and been praised for it, the valedictorian is invited to give it again, this time before the town's leading citizens at their club smoker. He is aware of differences between the graduation and the smoker. The first is a black ceremony in a familiar setting. We can assume that he has given many speeches and participated in many ceremonies at the school. The graduation will have been a typically sober, civilized ritual and therefore limited in its power to transport an audience. But the smoker is an elite function in a white sanctum to which he has never before been admitted. He is awed by the prospect of performing before powerful and dangerous figures, but he hardly anticipates the orgy ahead or the ordeals that he must pass before his initiatory rites are completed. The smoker, with its sport, sex, and drunkenness as well as the ritual narration which the boy will give, is a Dionysian spectacle. Like fraternal and professional conventions that are on the wild side, it is a ceremony of renewal; its main function is rejuvenation for the aging aristocracy of the town.

But the boy does not understand these things. The only thing that is important to him is to impress the dignitaries assembled. When, while waiting to recite, he is invited to participate in parts of the orgy (described below), he is confused. The invitation comes from the

---

* The distinction between stylization and individuality is an important one. Individuality derives from the lifelong accumulation of experiences, which are never the same in different people, even twins. Stylization means accentuation of limited elements of one's behavior. A highly stylized person may be striking, but little of his personality and experience is reflected in his behavior.

school superintendent, the same man who selected him to be valedictorian and then invited him to the smoker. Fearing to participate, he nevertheless tries, as usual, to do what is expected of him. As a result, he becomes part of a spectacle that is painful and humiliating, and by the time he gets to his oration he has been stripped of the dignity which he struggled so hard to maintain.

In speaking, he strains to regain a dignified image. His fervor returns as he gets into his oration; he becomes so caught up in his own solemnity that he does not notice at first that the revelers are only half listening to him. Their laughter and inattention spur him to raise his voice and put even greater emotional emphasis into it. Swallowing blood mixed with saliva, fighting nausea, he struggles on. There is no question of quitting, of not doing what he has been called upon to do. A well-schooled performer, our valedictorian stands in front of his mockers, using all his resources to maintain his ceremonial dignity. He manages to ignore his pain and fear, his disheveled appearance and the memory of humiliations just suffered. He finishes his oration.

The audience's response—thunderous applause—is more than he expects. What is he to make of this? Are the revelers serious or is their enthusiasm another joke? Despite their exploitation and humiliation of him, and despite the exaggeration of their applause, they do appreciate and approve of him. The evidence of their interest and faith in him is the college scholarship they then give him. The purpose of the invitation to the smoker had been to ratify their selection of him, and the ordeals were part of his initiation. The scholarship is his ticket for the next part of his journey.

Simple, consistent cruelty and rejection would have been easier for him to grasp, easier to integrate into a sense of who he was and where he belonged; they would have given him a foundation for dealing with life in the long run. But the treatment he has received from figures of authority is confusing. They were sincere in praising his stilted rhetoric and in exhorting him to future good deeds, but their ridicule was also real.

Many of our children are treated like candidates for leadership to some extent. They are conditioned to excel. We expect them to go to college and we often make sacrifices to pay their way. Yet when they have something serious to say we are apt to deride or patronize them. We laugh, sometimes insisting that we are laughing with them. Often we pretend to listen while our thoughts are on something else. When they perform we usually applaud and reward them extravagantly, with little discrimination as to merit or understanding of what the performance meant to them. We praise them for solemnly mouthing shallow, conventional slogans. We exhort them to follow ethical standards that we consider impractical or even irrelevant to our own lives. We urge them toward a superior morality. We encourage them to become heroes. And, without being clear about what we are doing, we also degrade them. If we become aware of our contradictory treatment of them we are embarrassed, for we are not deliberately using such treatment as preparation for leadership. We have forgotten that the degradation and elevation are vestigial symbols of death and deification in traditional initiation rites. Not knowing what we are doing, we are likely to foster confusion in our children to the extent that they depend on us to define their roles and identities.

When it is hard for a child to know whether his elders are honoring him or making fun of him, he will be confused as to what aspects of himself are valued. However, some lessons can be learned without understanding. Solemnity can be taken seriously by a serious audience; it also can be made fun of. Exaggerated speech and gestures can similarly be taken seriously or laughed at. Thus histrionic style may be rewarded under varied conditions and adopted for use whenever a performance is asked for. We are assuming that the subject is strongly enough motivated to please and is willing to be laughed at. If he submits to requests that require performance under embarrassing conditions, he will have little dignity. But if his function is ceremonial, requiring only a semblance of dignity, he will become adept at simulating it. He will be able to protect his own feelings to an extent by not recognizing them and by becoming impervious to his audience. Thus children who are brought up to perform are likely to develop adaptations that are self-alienating.

THE PEEPHOLE

In Greece displays of sex were designed to promote fertility of the fields and women and to inspire the public. In the Roman arena sex seems to have been used more to gratify sadistic and masochistic interests of a jaded audience. Morale building, titillation, and the freeing of pent-up primitive drives are the functions of part of the smoker, during which a white woman, naked, performs a voluptuous dance as the men watch. The valedictorian is made to watch also, very much aware that he, too, is being watched. He wonders whether he is expected to look at her or away; should he enjoy the sight of her body or would that anger the whites? His emotions are confused, and the clues in the faces of the white men are ambiguous.

The invitation to watch is clear enough, but he has already learned to be wary of traps. He has also learned to suppress impulses and emotions. The lesson learned by his ancestors on the plantation has been passed on. House boys (an elite compared to field hands) were thrust routinely by their position into the presence of dancing, carousing, flirting, or partly dressed white women. And decorum required that they act as if they were blind, impassive, and impotent. House boys did not, of course, cease to exist after the Emancipation. And in public, black males have been provided with a display of beckoning heroines, sirens, and advertising models who were white until recent years. With live women, especially in the South, the game of "Look, but don't touch!" was a tense and tricky one. Blacks were aware of being watched and were occasionally reminded that if their glances were construed as leers they might be beaten or killed.

The boy at the smoker senses the hostility of the men, the harm they may do him if his attitude toward the woman displeases them. What he does not understand is that they derive sexual gratification from watching him look at the dancer, and that his dilemma is a reflection of theirs. The carousing dignitaries are playing a similar trick on themselves. Victims of a sexually stimulating and inhibiting culture, many of them wedded to frigid virgins whom the culture fostered, they use the smoker for partial release. In a carnival atmosphere they tantalize themselves and each other, expressing some of their forbidden desires. Part of the game is laughing at each other's reactions, mocking those who abandon themselves. Pain mixes into the pleasure; being teased, frustrated, and laughed at goes together with indulging in the forbidden. The more restrained ones participate vicariously through identification with those who let themselves go as well as with the entertainers.

For many of them, the black youth is a symbol of lust, an uninhibited animal with oversized genitals. He personifies the primordial, powerful urges which civilization is supposed to have stamped out of genteel people. He is the actor of what is repressed in themselves. By projecting themselves into him, their voyeuristic pleasure, sadism, and masochism, and their vicarious participation in the spectacle are heightened. (Their sexual interest in him is a more intense example of the fascination that society finds in the sexuality of youth.)

Our need to deal vicariously with conflicting sexual tendencies arises from some of the same sources as the valedictorian's dilemma does. In growing up, boys see mothers, aunts, and sisters dancing, carousing, flirting, necking, bathing, or dressing, and must pretend not to be aroused, learning to suppress fantasies and emotions as well as erections. We have all had opportunities to look at forbidden things, with the choice of looking away, aware that our looking might be observed and punished. Having repressed, displaced, and transformed early sexual conflicts to the extent that mothers and sisters are rarely recognized as even being capable of arousing them, males are generally in a state of vague sex frustration. "Look, but don't react!" is a feature of daily life.

THE ARENA

The battle of the gladiators was a Roman institution. Originating as part of a funeral ceremony, it may have had the initiatory function of enabling the deceased to enter his new life. But its main use became public entertainment.

The valedictorian has been under the impression that he was invited to the smoker because of his intellect and because he was special. It comes as a shock to him to be recruited for a battle royal,* treated as if he were any boy off the street who would fight for a few dollars. He is blindfolded and put in a ring with nine others. Inability to see multiplies his confusion and fear; it seems to him that he is being attacked from all sides. He struggles for a way to contend with this situation without forgetting his mission. Amid the anarchy in the ring, he tries to think of his speech. Not for a minute does he lose the awareness that he is in the presence of people who can seriously influence his future and that he must impress them properly.

At first the pressure is too much for him. Unable to see, he finds it difficult to control his movements. He stumbles about like a drunken man, fighting hysterically. However as the battle progresses he begins to understand it better and discovers that he can control it. His blind-

---

* The history of the battle royal as public spectacle is obscure. Continuing interest in it is shown by the frequent use of the melee scene, usually in a bar, in Western and other movies. A recent form is the demolition derby. Dozens of men (and, more recently, women) drive at each other in cars. They drive backwards much of the time, adding to the wildness of the conflict. The scene is one of apparent destructive fury without plan, in an arena which is soon piled with smoking wrecks. The winner is the survivor, the last driver able to keep his car running.

fold has been put on loosely; with effort he can see well enough to be able to aim his punches and elude his opponents. He does this craftily, not to make it apparent to the spectators that he is cheating. After a while victory is within his grasp, but he begins to worry if his hosts will think he has gone too far. While hesitating, he is knocked out.

The violence of the competition in the ring has been intensified by the actions of the spectators. Some of them become so excited that they nearly abandon their role as nonparticipants, cajoling, tempting, and threatening the fighters to greater mayhem. In their vicarious participation, the spectators identify with the gladiators. They have designed the game for their own pleasure, and it expresses their fantasies. The blind, reckless, animalistic conflict in the ring is a thinly disguised, vicarious act of the creatures in the seats.

These spectators, as well as spectators of boxing, wrestling, hockey, and football—our more openly violent games—are not essentially different from their Roman ancestors. Discussion of sports is usually focused on participants, ignoring spectators. The athletes are seen as the protagonists (often nobly), motivated primarily by a will to win. The game is seen as a "contest." The spectators are incidental to the main drama, as are a theater or television audience, in the traditional view. However, the point to be made here is that *the spectators are the prime movers of the scene*. The motivation of the boy is secondary in shaping the contest and its outcome. His purpose includes preserving some remnant of dignity, remembering his lines, impressing his elders, 'and avoiding being hurt. Uppermost in his mind is satisfying the spectators. Winning the fight is of little significance to him. Thus the fight consists in essence of a spectacle designed by the spectators and acted for them.

This idea is important as we become increasingly a nation of spectators. When that fact is mentioned, it is usually to stress the passivity and detachment of, for example, the man watching football on television Saturday and Sunday afternoons, who seems to be actively alienating himself from his family, as well as being hypnotized by a ritual repeated over and over before his eyes. His passivity and detachment are significant and do bear on the subject of alienation. But no less significant is the fact that the spectator, as the consumer for whom the sport is designed, is influencing and exploiting the athlete, and thereby contributing to the athlete's alienation.

The idea of staged spectacle is not new; professional wrestling, the most synthetic of our sports, has for years been officially and publicly recognized as an exhibition rather than as a fight or contest. The same applies to the roller derby; in both, the actors simulate violence far beyond that which inheres in them or in the game. Professionals are not as likely as the rest of us to be confused about whether they are being themselves or performing according to other people's scripts. But even actors have experienced serious difficulties arising from confusion between their roles and their selves. In the situation of high school and college athletes, clear signs as to what is role and what is self are lacking. Often the student is misdirected, as when he is told that his participation in school athletics is part of his education and thus *gives expression to his own need for physical fitness* and *character development,* and the public interest in spectacle is minimized.*

Taking the smoker as a whole, as experienced by the valedictorian, it is a series of sharply disjointed experiences; strong arousals are followed by degrading rebuffs; doors open in front of him while he becomes more painfully and self-consciously aware that he may not simply pass through them. It is a series of seductions without consummations.

In relation to a boy's development, such teasing is malignant. It encourages masochism to the extent that he tries to please. The adults obtain pleasure from the boy's embarrassment and pain. And it is the blending of sadism with benevolence that hinders him from clarifying his position in his own mind. He is a victim of the spirit of the men's club, which embodies the goals of being boys together and of doing good deeds.

The dignitaries at the smoker also play the role of parents. While the valedictorian is being taught his place, he is also being prepared for his future, for a new, more prestigious place. But that, too, is an alienating process. His elders have selected him and defined a special place for him. He cannot become one of them, and being chosen by them estranges him from his peer group. Being chosen leads in a number of ways to his becoming an outsider.

---

* The battle royal may also be interpreted as a caricature of competition in life (particularly in the business sphere). The blindfold is a symbol of innocence. We send our youth into the brutal arena that is life, but we send them blindfolded by a simple, unrealistic set of rules for human conduct. This blindfold is not impenetrable; as with other illusions, its power depends on the willingness of the subject to be blind and the strength of the taboo against peeking. Those of our children who are believers in the Ten Commandments, as well as the skeptics, have been exposed to reality. Like the valedictorian, they can see through the blindfold when they are ready to.

He does not yet understand these things. Despite his cunning and his distrust, he lacks experience and is not fully informed about what is planned for him. He has, of course, not been prepared for understanding; rather, he has been groomed for performance.

THE CAMPUS

Hazing of freshmen is a college tradition and ridicule is an essential part of it. A common reaction to hazing is increased self-consciousness and uncertainty about how to act. Hazing is largely impersonal, based on the subject's membership in a class rather than his individual traits. However freshmen who show eccentricity are tormented more than others. The main lesson is not to act in any way that draws attention to oneself or makes one appear different. Thus one seeks to walk from class to class in a group. One learns to laugh at the "right time," which is when others are laughing. The more intimidation and physical danger* in the hazing, the more self-conscious and calculated the actions of the subject become. In other words, he becomes highly self-conscious under conditions that penalize spontaneous, individualistic behavior and reward artificial conventionality.

On the campus, athletes have comprised a special class, with football players receiving the most glory. Their life has been an exaggeration of college life generally. Football recruits have undergone more persistent and brutal hazing than other freshmen, with more serious alienating effects, according to Shaw (1972).** For all freshmen, arrival at college meant entering an awesome and unfamiliar environment. The bewilderment of the football recruits was intensified by the special conditions of their induction. They were segregated on arrival and a scheduled routine occupied almost all of their time. Eating, sleeping, and talking was done in the company of teammates. Thus they could not escape the presence of the older players who tormented them.

Hazing seems to have come as a particular shock to some of the

---

* Occasional deaths from hazing are still reported.

** Systematic data on hazing and other experiences of college athletes are lacking. Shaw's observations and experiences as a football recruit plus interviews with former players are the source of his material. His data are limited to football at the University of Texas in the mid-1960s. The experiences described do not apply to most college athletes to the same degree, but they are common enough for consideration as an institutionalized way of treating football candidates at many colleges. As Sauer (1972) has pointed out, it would be a mistake to consider the University of Texas unique in its football practices.

football recruits. Shaw, like the others, had been a football star in high school. As a result he had been actively sought by the college with money, sexual enticement, and the promise of a superior education. During this courtship he had been encouraged to believe that the coaches had a strong personal interest in him. Therefore the neglect and indifference with which they left him to flounder on his arrival in a surprisingly hostile environment was a severe disappointment to him. (Throughout his four years he found the alternation of acceptance and rejection by coaches particularly baffling.) He found himself struggling with feelings of isolation and unreality.

Perhaps Shaw and his fellow recruits should not have been surprised at the treatment they received. Football is widely known as the major college sport; many schools are identified in the public eye more by the emphasis they give to football than by anything else. Football success is reputed to be all-important to a college's alumni, who in turn are a needed source of income. In addition, football stimulates the interest of students and faculty. It is usually a college's main spectator sport. Therefore it is understandable that college administrators attach importance to it and that football scholarships are awarded primarily to promote success of teams rather than to further educational interests of recipients. Shaw knew all these things. The basic elements of the contract were plain enough to him at the outset: he wanted the money and was offering the college a superior performance; the college wanted a winning team and was offering a scholarship. Of course there were major inequalities in the arrangement. Shaw at seventeen was new in dealing with colleges and had some of the innocence and idealism of youth. Whatever he had heard of college sports, he did not know the situation from experience. On the other hand, the coaches were professionals who had dealt with thousands of high school graduates. And, though they probably did not try hard to deceive him, their blandishments had a powerful effect on him because of his prior conditioning.

We are accustomed to think of injuries as incidental and regrettable side effects of athletics. In addition, injuries to key players are a handicap to team success. Therefore it may come as a shock to consider a training program that fosters injuries and then exploits them as part of a mental conditioning process. A high rate of injuries was an inevitable consequence of routine football practice, as described by Shaw. At the end of the first day of tackling practice for fifteen freshman linebackers, "there were a couple of broken bones, a broken nose, and a brain concussion. . . ." And for special disciplinary purposes there were special drills which were much more productive of injuries.*

Candidates for the team who were injured or ill, but not so seriously as to prevent them from coming to practice, were in an extreme bind. If they performed poorly they were criticized. And if they referred to their handicap as an excuse they were treated as malingerers. Sometimes they were given extra drills that were especially arduous and painful. And in general they were marked for humiliation by coaches in front of teammates.

An obvious adaptation to such treatment was to hide injuries and illnesses—to bear pain, fight exhaustion, and perform well enough to escape notice. If a player wanted medical attention for an injury, he was "required" to get permission from the team trainer. And permission was often denied. (One could consult a doctor without permission. Few did.)

To feel pain while being told by a figure of authority that one is not in pain puts one in a dilemma. If he is oriented toward pleasing his mentor and becoming what the mentor wants, he must deny or invalidate his own bodily sensations and needs. It is confusing to be told, in contradiction of a person's own perception, that he is not injured, not sick, not exhausted and not in need of care, but rather that he is making excuses, shirking, and lying. To do what is wanted requires more than hiding his awareness of himself; it requires him to make his bodily sensations and self-awareness irrelevant to his actions.

For athletes, body perceptions are particularly important. Shaw described how the atmosphere of physical competition among teammates made them highly conscious of their own bodies—of size, weight, thickness of forearms and legs. Their physical condition was essential to their function (second in importance only to their mental toughness). Thus they were in the bind of being overly concerned with their bodies while having to ignore how their bodies felt. Shaw's adaptation

---

* One example was having two players run at each other and collide at full speed. The traditional idea that athletics builds character as well as bodies is reversed in Shaw's picture. Players are damaged mentally and physically in order to provide athletic spectacle. (The more debilitating drills were for candidates for the team, not for regular players.) The option of quitting the team was, of course, available. But there was considerable social and economic pressure against quitting, some of it from the players' parents. Quitting usually meant losing one's scholarship; those who left the team were not likely to remain at college.

involved dissociating himself from his body. An extreme of this reaction was the perception of a part of his body as an object or possession rather than as self. This concept was fostered by the procedure of "beefing up," whereby an athlete's weight was increased to fit him for his football position.*

Modifying one's body for the sake of football makes sense if football is one's primary, definitive function in life. According to Shaw, football did define the candidates' lives. Girlfriends and social activities were discouraged and academic pursuits were subordinated to football. And coaches largely controlled candidates' lives. Regimentation is self-alienating because it makes people's behavior uniform, indiscriminate, and limited to a fraction of their potential. Football players were regimented more strictly and for a larger part of the day than were other students. Football so dominated their thoughts and conversation that they gave the impression of mental dullness and lack of interests.

To summarize, the candidates were subjected to a comprehensive mental conditioning process. Although only some of it was deliberate, incidental features fitted into the plan. The goals of the process were as follows (adapted from Shaw).

Defining manliness and worth as being a good player.
Developing total dedication, marked by:
unquestioning obedience,
unwavering physical courage,
an attitude of never quitting,
ability to take suffering,
self-denial.

With their identity heavily tied to the role of football hero, those who failed to make the team felt lost and ashamed. In some cases their shame lasted for years after leaving the campus. And failure was the

---

* For a description of a legendary hero who treated parts of his body as separable objects, see the Trickster in the next chapter. Shaw characterized himself as a trickster (practical joker). The Miami Dolphins, who set a professional football record in 1972 of winning all seventeen games and the championship, used weight control, in which players were assigned specific weights by coaches. In addition it was reported that some of the regulars played the entire season despite being injured. The effect of thinking of oneself and others as objects was illustrated in 1972 by two pitchers for the Yankees who exchanged families. In explaining their behavior, they mentioned the similarity of the families; each consisted of a wife, two small children, a dog, and a house.

prevalent experience; of the high school stars who held football scholarships, three-fourths did not last. Some dropped out by choice, but most struggled on and were eliminated by injuries or by the coaches.

The experience of the football candidates described above differs in degree and in some details from traditional college experience. Greatness has been the goal of many athletes; it has also been a goal of coaches in shaping them. Similarly, greatness has been the goal of our academic system, despite partial commitment to universal education. Although our public schools have been designed to admit all children, they have functioned largely as a system for selecting and channeling the minority who were expected to go on to college and to emerge as leaders. Vocational and commercial sidetracks were provided, but the main line went to the top. "For a long time all boys were trained to be President," said a school-board president a few decades ago (Goodman, 1970). Similarly college deans used to feel a clear responsibility to society, and students experienced the effects of it. When I went to college in the 1940s the dean welcomed us with a reminder of our special status. We were, he said, an elite. We had been chosen carefully for admission. But we were only candidates, and college was a proving ground. Fortifying his predictions of our future with ominous statistics, he said that only a quarter of us would graduate. Half would be eliminated by the end of our freshman year. But those who did survive the trials were destined to be leaders.

We learned in time that the hazing was much more than sadistic pranks to be endured; it was only part of an initiation that stripped us of our dignity, complacency, and individuality. We had thought that our prior experiences, especially in high school, had prepared us for college. But much of what we had learned was treated as an obstacle. As in traditional initiations, the first phase consisted of blurring our identities to make it easier to fit us into our new ones.

LEADERSHIP TRAINING

When he was seventeen and inexperienced, and his star was rising, Ellison's valedictorian thought he was being honored by the invitation to the smoker. Later, after a series of defeats, he concluded that he had been used. Similarly, at seventeen Shaw thought he was being honored in the eagerness of the college to have him, but later felt that he had been treated as less than human. The combination of elevation and degradation in the training of future leaders comes to us from older cultures where it was a more deliberate practice. Cultures in which princes were chosen by birth had worked out the training to a greater extent. Our future leaders are selected and trained by people who are not specifically versed in their task nor always conscious of what they are doing. They employ practices inherited from their predecessors and apply them to all students, not only the promising ones. Therefore the goals and philosophy of leadership training in earlier cultures may help us to understand alienating features of our schools.

In cultures in which leadership training was deliberate, the goal was often clearly dehumanizing. According to an old Hindu theory of government (Watts, 1966), a prince's "first rule is that he must trust no one and be without a single intimate friend." The price to be paid in attaining this extreme of isolation was justified by the view that a prince existed to serve his people and that his personal needs were irrelevant. Freedom to act on his emotions and impulses was out of the question. Shakespeare made a number of distinctions between princes and others in *Hamlet* (Act I, Scene 3). The teenage Ophelia was advised that she could only be hurt by loving the Prince. She protested that he loved her, but that fact was brushed aside. Whether Hamlet loved her or not was irrelevant because he was a prince and therefore not free to enter into a relationship based on emotions or personal and selfish considerations (". . . his will is not his own. . . . He may not . . . Carve for himself . . ."). The advice, "to thine own self be true," is only for free men. Hamlet was a prince and could not be true to himself. Francis Bacon (1891) argued similarly:

> *Men in great place are thrice servants—servants of the sovereign or State, servants of fame, and servants of business; so that they have no freedom, neither in their persons . . . [nor] actions. . . . It is a strange desire to seek power and to lose liberty, or to seek power over others, and to lose power over a man's self.*

People who sacrifice their personal lives to serve others are often thought of as possessing moral strength and faith. However Machiavelli (1940) excluded such inner resources from the character of an ideal leader. To be a good prince, he said, one should exhibit the customary virtues of his society (such as fidelity, integrity, religiosity) without fully possessing them. Machiavelli did not mean that a prince should pretend; rather he advocated habitual sincerity in the expression of virtuous sentiments. But the sincerity proposed was superficial, on a level with greeting-card sentiment, and thus far short of the faith or inner commitment that might sustain an isolated person.

Translated into more precise psychological language, Machiavelli's dictum is as follows. A leader should act so that others perceive him as virtuous, and he should perceive himself so. He should behave in a virtuous manner naturally (i.e., from habit, not by deliberation) whenever the situation calls for such behavior. But when community interests are served by action that goes against the virtues, the leader should be responsive to community interests and not limited by virtues. In other words, his virtuous responses should be limited to those stimulus situations in which important matters are not at stake.

With such traditional ideals of leadership in mind, we can see an orientation which training would logically assume. To condition a child to distrust people we would invite his trust and betray him repeatedly. Such treatment would also promote avoidance of intimacy on his part. To condition him not to act on his instincts and feelings we would deny him satisfaction when he does so and reward him for ignoring his inner urgings. And to condition values on a par with the rules of etiquette we would reward virtue when superficial and conventional and punish adherence to principle in serious matters. If we consider child-rearing in the home and school, many details that fit the above pattern will come to mind. In many ways our culture, with its competitive and pragmatic orientation, fosters distrust, emotionless efficiency, and superficial values.

To summarize the process of preparation and induction of leaders as illustrated in the experiences of the valedictorian and the football recruit, it involves disjointed experiences. Seduction alternates with rebuff; honor is combined with degradation. And, though these experiences arouse pain and embarrassment, the candidate is discouraged from attending to his feelings. The following alienating effects have been mentioned.

Becoming a mouthpiece for the ideas of others
Fitting oneself to a life role which belongs to someone else in the sense that it fulfills the other's wishes and fantasies
Developing shallow adherence to the values of one's culture
Becoming confused about one's place
Being removed from one's peer group as a consequence of being chosen for a special role

Suppressing one's wishes and emotions as a consequence of being
stimulated under conditions of menacing scrutiny
Making one's sensations and needs irrelevant to one's behavior
Developing self-denial, unquestioning obedience, and dedication
Learning to maintain an appearance of innocence and to deny
awareness of reality
Learning to perform without understanding one's role
Having one's worth defined narrowly

An opportunist derives a number of advantages from learning to
control his feelings. By suppressing his eagerness and his expectations,
he is not as easily seduced and his disappointments are muted. In
addition, suppressing and manipulating his own feelings enables him
better to act in a way that pleases others. Suppression of instincts and
feelings frees him to operate on the basis of what he can see and calcu-
late—to become an efficient computer. The shrewd child reads between
the lines, learning the ropes, becoming a sensitive observer of his
elders' wishes and of their sensitivities. At first the skills he develops
and the knowledge he obtains enable him to avoid rubbing his elders
the wrong way, giving him advantages over his peers. Should he continue his rise toward the top, he will use his skills increasingly to manipulate his elders as well.

What this kind of child believes is likely to be complex. Sometimes he deliberately restrains his instincts and bides his time, so that
he will be in the right place when he is strong enough to take what
he wants. Sometimes he sincerely wishes to please his elders. Commonly he is doing both, being neither a complete opportunist nor a
complete fool, but not being fully aware of the discrepant sides of
himself. For example, in school he is the one who knows how things
are done and is quick to pick up the idiosyncrasies of his teachers.
He learns what is wanted and in what manner it is to be packaged.
And when he delivers it he is likely to believe that the product is
worthwhile and that his teacher has a right to want it.

The main point here is that, to the extent that he puts others'
feelings ahead of his own, to the extent that *he makes his own feelings
irrelevant to his actions,* he is not developing an identity; but he is
developing the characteristics of a traditional hero.

The special training given the leadership candidate is offered increasingly to youth. In the past, those marked for greatness were few
in number in most high schools. But now, with our unprecedented

affluence, most high school students are considered potential candidates for college and what lies beyond. They generally are expected to aspire to creative, meaningful work and to success. These goals are promoted as worthy in our society and they are held out as accessible to all. The means to achieve them are made increasingly available; free education plus scholarships, loans and work-study programs have opened college doors to more of the poor. With our equalitarian creed, our theoretical classlessness and social mobility (even if they are not realized), relatively few youngsters are *considered* necessarily out of the running. Very few are not exposed to indoctrination about possibilities ahead of them. This fact is emphasized by comparing the horizons of a typical American child with the horizons of a typical child in an impoverished or heavily caste-structured nation—by comparing our childrens' possibilities with those of the great majority growing up in most nations, especially in past centuries. A situation of opportunity and encouragement plus frustration and humiliation particularly fosters the problems that concern us here. And it is the expanding horizon, the growth of freedom, and the loosening of barriers that have made increasing numbers eligible for such initiations.

INVISIBILITY

For most candidates the path does not lead to the top. People drop out at different points along the road upward, but the dropout rate has been very high in college. The campus beckons powerfully and provides ordeals few can pass without damage to their sense of self. Ellison (1953) used the concept of invisibility to describe the alienation of those who drop all the way out, hitting bottom. His valedictorian emerges from the smoker with increased suspiciousness of people and confusion about how to act. At college he relies heavily on passivity, deference, and conventionality. When these fail him, he tries other ways to find his place, turning to unusual and violent means as his frustration mounts. He becomes a rebel, but leading a successful revolution is possible for very few; like most young militants he fails. He then drops out entirely. Having tried to work his way in, sneak in, wheel and deal himself in, and batter his way in, he is left finally with no more values to go by. He becomes the most extreme of outsiders, an underground creature, a shadow. He removes himself from society, like the unemployed, homeless ones whom we do not count in our census and pretend not to notice on the street. But he also has become less than human to himself, seeing himself at times more as a phantom than a person.

Having given up dealing with society and its institutions and members, he no longer needs to concern himself with people's trustworthiness. But in his isolation, problems in distinguishing between fantasy and reality become greater than ever.* His tenuous sense of existence occupies him more and more. When people pass him on the street he scrutinizes them for a sign that they are aware of him and examines himself for a sensation of contact. Most people pass him without recognition. Presumably they are sufficiently aware of his presence to avoid him. With these gentler people he feels no contact whatever. Others, not seeing him or pretending not to, jostle him or bump into him and move on as if he were nothing.

Earlier, when he had been more socialized, he preferred gentle people; they, at least, did not hurt or insult him in an obvious way. Now, having lost his sense of reality, he sometimes looks for the rough ones—the bumpers. They enable him to experience his anger as part of an interpersonal encounter rather than in the abstract. They provide the possibility for him to be in emotional contact with someone and *feel* more alive, if only for a moment. More important is the hope that one day the bump will be so hard that it cannot be ignored. The Invisible Man will then *become* real to a real person, and thereby real to himself. His need for recognition is becoming an overriding one.

The violent encounter—the bump—takes on unusual significance for one who cannot distinguish between reality and fantasy. It appeals to the underground man, whose life is a nightmare, agonizing and unreal. It appeals especially as a solution to one who has exhausted other means of escape from limbo. A casual dreamer seeks a pinch, a piece of violence to resolve his uncertainty, to make him feel aware and awake (which implies being alive). The prisoner in a perpetual nightmare needs the pinch more than anything. And as minor violence proves ineffective he prepares to escalate, to come to the ultimate wager.

At the verge of risking his life, only fear can deter him. Conscience has become irrelevant. "To whom can I be responsible?" cries the Invisible Man. And he resentfully adds, "And why should I be, when you refuse to see me?" (Ellison, 1953). More serious is the ques-

---

* Fromm-Reichmann (1959) noted that the ability to distinguish between subjective self and external environment is undermined by loneliness and isolation.

tion of what responsibility a nonperson can have. One who is quite isolated may find that values and responsibility do not exist as abstractions. A person who is totally isolated lives without norms (which derive from prevalent behavior patterns) or commandments (which involve a relationship between a subject and an authority). He may try to live by imaginary norms and commandments, but under conditions of uncertain identity and reality his imagination becomes confused. As Ellison pointed out, an extremely estranged person finds that alternatives like good and evil or honesty and dishonesty shift amorphously and distinctions between them vanish. A totally isolated person is an amoral one. (We are apt to consider him immoral, for we retain standards to judge him by.)

Fearing to risk his tenuous existence, an extremely alienated person may choose to walk softly, unobtrusively, stepping aside where necessary to maintain a marginal existence, one which many of our youth as well as existentialist philosophers call non-existence. An alternative is to try to become real by seeking confrontation. Like Hamlet's choice, to act or to go on sleeping translates into *to be or not to be.* There is no confrontation without tension and risk.

Two methods of confrontation, with the goal of clarifying status and thereby reducing alienation, are antisocial behavior (explored in Chapter 4) and ritual (Chapter 5).

□ 4. THE LOW ROAD

College students have long been known for acts of defiance: lampooning their elders, smearing paint or filth on statues, or defacing hallowed buildings. Some acts of defiance are intended as serious social protest, but society prefers to view them as pranks. Amused or irritated indulgence is a common reaction, although society occasionally erupts in anger. In 1970 students at Kent State University engaged in a demonstration. Guardsmen came on campus and, although the students were not violent, became hysterical and killed some of them. Many people felt that the students had gotten what they deserved.

The severity of the reaction against the students by both public and members of the Guard suggests a peculiar and intense relationship. Partly it is because parents place their hopes in students that they readily feel betrayed and punitive. Another element in the anger is bafflement. Many things which young people do lightly strike others as senseless and even cruel rather than funny. Casual defiance or contempt of authority arouses uneasiness. More unnerving is what appears as a readiness by youth to abuse or even mutilate their own bodies and minds. Their clothing and hairstyles sometimes seem to elders unattractive to the degree of being disfiguring. Carelessness about sex and pregnancy, inattention to school work, and dropping out raise the spectre of a ruined future. Drugs, when used by youth, bring to mind risks to health, sanity, and even life. Lack of concern about consequences to others and to oneself disturbs parents. The most alarming thing is the willingness of militant youth to destroy and to be destroyed.

Pranks, violation of taboos, destructive and self-destructive acts, seen occasionally in most young people, are a way of life for some people. Mostly young and bright, they are called psychopaths.* Among their talents is exceptional skill in pleasing and impressing people. They dazzle us, but not for long. We hardly begin to think of them as heroes before their acts become despicable to us. It is in their own eyes that they remain heroes; many see themselves vaguely as engaged in a redemptive mission, but in society's view they are destroyers rather than saviors. A grudging admiration is sometimes accorded these "evil geniuses," and occasionally they are seen as superhuman in their cleverness. But the more general, explicit view of society is that they are contemptible and subhuman. Often they are called criminal psychopaths, for it is in their breaking of the law that they come to our attention. However, they may be generally antisocial—mischievous, cruel, exploiting, destructive—without necessarily doing illegal things. Antisocial behavior is what strikes us about them. We may not notice that it is their alienation which is extreme and sets them apart from other people and criminals. They are alienated from society as individuals, not as members of any group. Although they defy authority, we do not think of them as political rebels. They seem so disconnected from any culture as to have nothing against which to revolt. Lindner (1944) called them rebels without a cause.

We can understand a man who steals money when he is out of work and his family is in urgent need of it. But we cannot understand the person who steals something he does not need, especially when he risks serious consequences in the process. And we cannot understand someone who steals things which he could easily get in other ways. Such a man seems more dangerous than one who commits crimes prudently for gain. The man who kills out of hatred or to fur-

---

* Other psychiatric names include psychopathic personality, antisocial personality, and sociopath. Prankishness is not usually listed in texts as a characteristic of psychopaths, but is commonly mentioned in describing them. Gouster, in 1878, listed delight in michief among the criteria for diagnosing them (cited in McCord and McCord, 1964). Good looks, cited as characteristic by Thorne (1967), is mentioned occasionally by others.

ther a cause seems human, but the one who kills without much reason and who risks capture or death for a whim does not. Apprehension and repugnance have been common reactions in scientists and clinicians as well as the public to the psychopath.

By considering someone subhuman, a barrier is created against understanding him; science has contributed little to our knowledge of the psychopath in 2500 years. Thus a major part of the problem in understanding him is our very reaction to him. A distorted perception is not simply an error to be corrected. The nature of the distortion may be considered a clue to the relationship between the psychopath and his community, reflecting needs in the community to which the role of psychopath is a response. Therefore traditional concepts about the nature of the psychopath, despite their inaccuracy, seem relevant to understanding his condition. The idea that his role is a response to society's needs can be seen in the psychopathic figures who are heroes in our folklore and myth—the sanctified outlaws, tricksters, and other anti-heroes of our culture. Their role is discussed later in the chapter.

THEORIES ABOUT A NONPERSON

In early times the psychopath was called uncivilized, asocial, and immoral. "Tribeless, lawless, heartless" said Aristotle (1943), taking the words from Homer, and calling the psychopath "an isolated piece." Aristotle argued that all men are born with a social instinct, and therefore an unsocial being could not be a man; he had to be either a beast or a god. Not receiving the benefit of the doubt, he was called "the most unholy and the most savage of animals." Social deficit was the critical element; antisocial behavior was the result.

Later, moral deficit was emphasized more than social. Psychopaths were said to lack consciences. By the nineteenth century, psychiatrists were diagnosing a condition called "moral insanity" or "moral imbecility." And the term "constitutional psychopathic inferior" suggested that the lack of conscience was inborn, a view still current. It was often thought that psychopaths were intellectually inferior, but the opposite idea was also common. With the rise of intelligence testing in this century, the psychopath's brightness was confirmed. His behavior, especially when bizarre, was sometimes considered due to insanity. America's best-known authority on psychopaths, Cleckley (1964), argued this position vigorously. However the prevalent view is still that the psychopath is fully rational.

In recent times clinicians began to find that psychopaths do have moral values or consciences. What they seemed not to have was anxiety, and that lack was used to explain the senseless, antisocial acts. In Freudian theory and in traditional views of discipline and social control, anxiety is seen as a deterrent to action. Stated simply, anxiety, derived from past punishments or threats, is aroused in anticipation of a forbidden act and hinders us from carrying it out. If our motive outweighs our anxiety we may carry out the act, but we are likely to worry beforehand and feel guilty afterward. Anxiety deters us; and if we go ahead anyway, anxiety plagues our efforts.

Some theorists have felt that a psychopath lacks the anxiety that makes conscience or anticipation of consequences effective. Therefore, he is not deterred. Even trifling motives may be sufficient for him to commit serious crimes. He can carry them off smoothly and coolly, untroubled by guilt afterward. Many of us have occasional moments when we seem indifferent to our convictions and to consequences, and do things we would not do at other times. Special circumstances foster such behavior, as at stag parties, fraternity initiations, or national conventions. In addition, moods like intoxication or despair have the effect of dulling the pricks of conscience or the anticipation of consequences. Thus occasional circumstances and moods enable us to do some things with unaccustomed detachment. For the psychopath, however, such dulling and detachment seemed to be the usual thing.*

If psychopaths lacked social instincts, consciences, or anxiety, they could be master criminals. With their established intelligence, if they lacked emotional reactions that deter people from engaging in taboo behavior, they would always be in a position to act in a calculated way. By considering an action only in relation to its probable consequences, they would also fit an ideal of rational man. Not only could they be super-criminals, they could be superior at any task or job. Scruples, sentimentality, loyalty, convention, or fear would not hold them back. They would neither equivocate nor procrastinate. They would be models of efficiency.

Immediately we see that by traditional views, psychopaths fit an ideal to which many people have aspired. Thus the image of the psychopath represents aspirations of people who have felt limited or trapped by emotion, conscience, and ties. It also follows that people

---

* However, recent reviews contradict the reported absence of anxiety—see Robins (1967), Bromberg (1961), or Teitelbaum (1965).

who lack conscience and anxiety could take the risks and violate the taboos that make heroes in the mythical tradition.

BONNIE AND CLYDE AND MR. HYDE

The heroic side of our image of the psychopath has not received much attention because of our preoccupation with his "evil" side. The monster of old movies has his counterpart in textbooks. One only has to read a few pages of Cleckley's (1941) monograph to see his distaste for the subjects of his study. Scientific descriptions of psychopaths have been derived from clinical observations and data supplied by law enforcement officers and exasperated relatives. As Bromberg (1961) noted, "the diagnostician necessarily sits in the seat of judgment" and the diagnosis of psychopathic personality "reflects social attitudes toward non-conforming individuals." The viewpoint of the clinical psychologist and psychiatrist, trained to think in terms of abnormality, is known for its negative bias—we are aware of the paradox that, although "normal" means average, the average person is often found to be abnormal by psychologists and psychiatrists. Similarly we recognize in the legal and penal system a tendency to focus on a person's faults. Neither has the psychopath helped to soften or broaden our one-sided picture of him by what he has said to us. However, he was on the defensive when we accosted him in the jail or when he came to our consulting room under court order, and we often made him more so by our demand that he account for his behavior. We have seen the face he puts on when confronted or cornered: wary, deceptive, sometimes insolent and mocking. But we have rarely seen the face which he turns to his best friend (when he has one).

Bonnie and Clyde showed that face. This was a movie about two actual people who became known to the public by their criminal exploits and were taken into the hearts of poor and dispossessed Americans of forty years ago as folk heroes. Bonnie and Clyde, companions and occasionally lovers, were portrayed as they appeared to each other. The movie has been criticized for glorifying them, but there was no glory in it. (Their elevation as heroes was not included in the movie.) For an American film of the 1960s it was fairly free of sentimentality, and no extenuation was offered for the crimes—none whatever. The film departed from the Hollywood pattern of pseudo-explanations of adult misbehavior on the basis of childhood experiences. Bonnie and Clyde were presented without childhoods, pasts, justification, or adornment. They were shown living brief, meager lives desperately. Their end was an utterly wretched death.

Clyde did not fit the stereotype of the psychopath; he was far from being tough and unfeeling. Easily hurt, shy, nervous, he hesitated to undertake things, especially when alone. These qualities were overshadowed by his bravado. But the film reminded us from time to time of the other side of his bravado—the fear and desperation.

Shyness, fear, and even desperation are commonplace. What distinguished Clyde was the barrenness of his life. Most of the things we live by had little meaning to him: parents, children, home, job, community activities, clubs, culture, athletics, hobbies. He was not bound to institutions, creeds, or property, nor limited by them. He had no future and, therefore, no reason to engage in the multitude of future-oriented daily chores that comprise the bulk of our lives. It is more than poetic to say that he had no past or future, and few ties to the present.

These facts are enough to serve as a beginning for explaining his behavior. His condition was conducive to monotony. Our daily life contains a great many acts and experiences that are repetitious, senseless, and unrewarding in themselves. Their meaning and value derive from their future consequences or from their being steps in a sequence, where the sequence has meaning as a whole, where the end of the sequence brings something new or worthwhile. Monotony is a condition of repetition without significant endings; sequences simply begin again. To illustrate this point in a different way, imagine that you are going to die tomorrow. Which of today's activities remain worth doing? Imagine also that you have no children or achievements or ideas to leave behind, nor any expectation of a future life. Imagine that you have no ties to anyone or anything that will remain when you are dead. Then the things that remain worth doing today are those that bring satisfaction today. Other things lose their meaning, becoming neutral if not burdensome. Expectations are what enliven acts that are otherwise monotonous. Depressing prospects make for a dreary routine.

When most of one's acts are no longer gratifying, the remaining few take on added importance. With monotony stretching out in all directions, opportunities to obtain a lift, a kick, become especially inviting. Similarly, when achievement in life is not available, little victories become valuable. Clyde was one who lived for the minor skirmishes and for the thrills and victories in them.

Because his ties were few and limited and his prospects nil, his freedom of action in any situation was considerable. He was not encumbered by assets that could be lost or by hopes whose future realization could be jeopardized. At any moment he had little to call his own, and therefore little to lose. For these reasons, Clyde was one who grasped at opportunities, even when they were slight. He readily risked what he had. He was a gambler.

Despite the simplicity of the movie portrait of Clyde, there were many who found it unacceptable and insisted on simplifying it further. They complained about Clyde's impotence and lack of interest in sex—a briefly illuminated aspect of his relationship with Bonnie. Similarly, they tended to edit the movie for themselves by forgetting Clyde's shyness, his nervousness before entering a bank, and his hesitancy and fear generally, and they misread his bravado for callousness. In short, they screened out his neurotic (therefore human) features. They tried to simplify him into an insensitive, hard creature, much as psychologists and psychiatrists have traditionally done with psychopaths.*

Similarly, many people would prefer that Hitler's biography show him as an animal without tender or human qualities. His gentleness, his ascetic abstention from alcohol, tobacco, meat, and marriage have not been taken seriously. Many people would rather believe that, like a demon, he will be found living some place than that he committed suicide. With a preference for seeing Hitler and Clyde as nonhuman, their private lives must come as a shock. We readily accept the Bonnie and Clyde of sensational newspaper accounts, the Hitler of propaganda and caricature. We are unwilling to see them as they appeared to someone who loved them.

Why the unwillingness? It seems that we are wary of being asked to forgive or condone something unacceptable, something we feel impelled to condemn. Accompanying this wariness is the fear that sociologists and psychologists, in their zeal for understanding people, have gone to the extreme of indulgence which promotes antisocial behavior. The argument may be sketched as follows. If we recognize

---

* The absence of neurotic traits used to be listed as a criterion of psychopathic personality. Cleckley (1964) went so far as to say, "There is nothing at all odd or queer about him, and in every respect he tends to embody the concept of a well-adjusted, happy person. . . . Everything about him is likely to suggest . . . robust mental health." However recent reports suggest the opposite (e.g., Robins, 1967).

that they are human, we may be led to understand and forgive them. If we forgive them, they will not be deterred from repeating their crimes. If we do not deter these people, what will prevent others from following suit? "Permissiveness"—loosely defined and equated with abdication of responsibility—is seen to be pulling down the shaky structure of society and letting chaos in.*

Without strong deterrents, what is to prevent others from following suit? What is to prevent the public generally from acting like psychopaths? This question seems at the root of the argument. It assumes that in all of us, inside us in some primitive part, lies dormant the propensity to rob and kill and rape. Paradoxically, the argument assumes what it denies: *under the idea that psychopaths are nonhuman is the idea that we are all psychopathic inside and that only a thin line of social deterrents holds back our rapaciousness.* Those who deny the human side of the psychopath are secret believers that Bonnie and Clyde and Hitler and Eichmann and the rest of us are brothers under the skin.

If we are all killers, it seems best not to know it. There is a fear that if people become aware of their antisocial impulses they may carry them out. Therefore a way of controlling impulses is to deny their existence. A parent who is infuriated by something his child has done says, "I'm not angry and I'm not trying to hurt you. I love you. That is why I have to teach you what is right." The child who sees anger and feels pain, but is told that he is receiving discipline or education, may question his own perceptions and emotions. A similar effect occurs when a parent says to a child who has assaulted someone or destroyed something, "You didn't mean that. It's not Tommy who did that. Tell mommy that you didn't mean it!" If the child did mean it, his dilemma is an obvious one.

The lesson of the story of Eden is that ignorance is bliss. As long as they remained unaware of their sexuality, Adam and Eve led a

---

* Forgiveness and condemnation are concepts with religious roots, involving good and evil. Scientific understanding (as distinct from compassionate understanding) has to do with causes and effects. Thus forgiveness and scientific understanding have little to do with each other, and when they come together in personal relationships the result is often confusing.

The fear of escalation indicated above seems to derive from cautionary determinism in Western thought which can be seen in the story of the Garden of Eden. The moral is: Beware of taking the first step. Before that step one is thought to have free will; afterward he is no longer in control. Beware of an early sex experience; it leads to prostitution. Beware of the first drink; it leads to alcoholism.

good and happy life. This type of argument is still commonly applied to the control of sexual impulses. Opponents of sex education in the schools believe that if children are permitted to learn that they possess sexual appetites and capacities, they will start exercising them prematurely and indiscriminately. Victorian culture carried such logic to an extreme: to deter girls and women from sexual indulgence, they were reared to be unaware of their desires.

This kind of denial is typically discriminatory and leads to scapegoating. Victorians did not say that all women lacked sex drives, but only that normal ones lacked it. They distinguished logically and set apart socially a class of sexual females—considered perverts or possessed by devils—whose sexuality was exaggerated and distorted. Thus a small group of women was caricatured and considered inhuman in order to deny the sexuality of the main group. (Actually both groups were dehumanized by the process.) The "abnormal" group was also exploited sexually and punished. But primarily they were scapegoats whose function was the preservation of the moral status of those women who constituted the cornerstone of family life.

The psychopath, when seen in the image of Mr. Hyde, personifying the evil of unrestrained instinct, is also a scapegoat. By setting him apart as an immoral creature, we seek to deny our unacceptable impulses. By thus ridding ourselves of evil and by punishing him we are attempting to control disturbing tendencies in ourselves.

THE DARK HERO

The argument that the image of the psychopath expresses society's unconscious needs has been suggested by writers who have attributed heroic functions and noble qualities to him. Dostoyevsky suggested that criminals serve as scapegoats by taking on themselves the guilt of the rest of society; he saw them as redeemers (Freud, 1959). Slochower (1961), in drawing a parallel between delinquents and heroes, saw criminality as basic to the hero's function. He stressed destructive and illegal acts as the very ones which serve to transform a decadent community. And Franz Alexander saw psychopaths as "born heroes who are predestined to a tragic fate" (Halleck, 1967).

The public has long associated criminality with creative genius. Henderson found character structure to be much the same in many psychopaths and geniuses.* Some writers have suggested that the only difference between a psychopath and a genius lies in *what we choose to emphasize about them.* Thus Bernard Shaw said that we judge the artist by his highest moment and the criminal by his lowest (Wilson, 1960). Many writers have portrayed the artist as a borderline criminal. Slochower argued that the rebellious impulses that move the psychopath to crime are the same ones that move the artist, who expresses them in the behavior of the hero whom he creates. Turning the coin, Kozol (1961) said, "Men of genius, with their creations and achievements subtracted, would undoubtedly be diagnosed as psychopaths."

Therefore the psychopath who has the idea that he is a special person engaged in a mission is not alone in his view of himself. In addition he can point to a position which is established for him in literature and folklore, a position which shows that his role is needed and appreciated. Psychopaths resemble traditional heroes in a number of ways. They are homeless wanderers who aimlessly get involved in dangerous adventures. They are intelligent, resourceful, and quick-thinking in difficult situations. They are men of action. Their ability to impress and inspire people is considerable, as are their courage and recklessness. They are ready to destroy people and things and to give up their own lives. And they are alienated from self and society. These are not enough similarities to equate them with heroes generally, but they do fit into a subclass of dark heroes.

How much the psychopath does for the benefit of others is not clear. Clinicians exchange stories of his "surprising" acts of service. As an older prisoner and repeater he often tries to save the youthful first offender, to turn him away from the empty, senseless life of crime and punishment. In the hospital he befriends helpless ones: he wheels cripples around, gets things for the bedridden, gives guidance to the naively forlorn, and fights for decent treatment and privileges for the weak. However these stories have not been collected systematically. Cleckley (1964) and others explained away such behavior as insincere and manipulative, designed to gain the psychopath's own ends. But this dismisses the service too quickly. Kesey's (1962) fictional account of mental hospital life features as its hero a man diagnosed as a psychopath. His character and how he is drawn from his isolation into

---

* Henderson (1939) was our best-known authority on psychopaths before Cleckley. See also McCord and McCord (1964) on the relation between the psychopath and the genius.

involvement with others, ending by sacrificing himself, present a puzzle which goes beyond Cleckley's formulation. Kesey's hero may seem improbable, but he has many counterparts in fiction and biography, in modern legend and ancient myth. Thus our culture provides antisocial models for incorporation into parents' fantasies about their children, models which can also serve as ideals for youth to follow.

The strength of the public desire for criminal heroes is shown by the speed with which Billy the Kid became an object of legend and worship in the Southwest.*

The redeemer who is a criminal, misfit, or prankster has varied forms. The best-known line of antisocial heroes is found in picaresque novels and biographies, which go back to Roman times. Their typical hero is a wandering rogue who exploits people and society generally with his tricks. His purposes are not consciously noble. But in holding society up to contempt he exposes it. Thus his life has an indirect redeeming function. (His is a kind of life psychopaths can identify with. Many feel that their lives serve to expose society; some want to publish their biographies in the public interest.) Sometimes the outlaw-hero's activities take on a deliberately noble purpose and his pranks are fairly good-natured, as in some legends of Robin Hood. On the other hand he may be a miserable wanderer whose misadventures make him as much a victim as those whom he intends to victimize. "His jests are often pointless, more often brutal; he indulges, when opportunity offers, in scurrility and obscenity," as in the legend of Till Eulenspiegel (Robertson, 1940). The latter type most resembles our stereotype of the psychopath.

THE TRICKSTER

The Trickster is a mythical deity who closely resembles psychopathic humans. Radin (1972) considered him a universal figure. Loki (Nordic), Hermes and Prometheus (Greek), and Mercury (Roman) are

---

* Billy the Kid is an excellent example of a psychopathic Oedipal hero. Stretching Raglan's twenty-two features of the hero myth, Adler (1951) found all of them in Billy's legend. Billy's history is also interesting in relation to the concept of Jocasta mothering. From early childhood he lived alone with his mother, with whom he was very close. Her life was pitiable, a sharp comedown from her cultured beginnings. When only nine, he killed a man who insulted her, and later he became the protector of another woman who had lost her husband. Thus deeds of service were mingled with callous killing in his reputation. And he was known, among other things, as Billy the Scapegoat. Jesse James' legend also fits the standard hero myth in a number of ways.

among the best-known examples. Radin's analysis of the Trickster in American Indian myth, from which the following is adapted, lends itself to psychological interpretation of the significance of dark heroes.

The Indian Trickster is an amorphous, shifting form. Although divine, he is also human and animal. His powers are extraordinary but his mentality is primitive and childish. As his Indian name indicates, he is known by his pranks; "Laughter, humour and irony permeate everything Trickster does" (Radin, 1972). But his pranks are often quite cruel and have no point except to satisfy a passing whim or to gain revenge for a minor insult. In a Winnebago version,* he kills and eats a number of children without hesitancy or regret. His interests are few; they center around his mouth, anus, and oversized penis. He has no morality, no sensitivity to others' feelings, and no fear or other emotions in the early part of his career. He is a violator of all taboos. He is also a schlemiel, often the victim of his own pranks; but he hardly minds the injuries he receives or inflicts on himself, even when they are serious. Unsuited to domesticity or responsibility and having little interest in people, he is a perpetual wanderer. He relies on cunning to get what he wants: clever tricks, lies, flattery, and disguise. But he lacks wisdom and his naiveté is extraordinary. Thus he follows no life plan, taking things as they come, falling victim to others' dares. By what he does and what he lacks, he is a typical psychopath. Thus it may surprise us that Indians viewed him indulgently as unfortunate and amusing rather than evil. (They also viewed him with awe, for he was a culture hero and deity.) The Trickster's life is significant in a number of ways.

> He is a creator, giver, and protector as well as a destroyer. Although he only occasionally does things that are directly beneficial to mankind, some of his misadventures also have good effects.** He is a scapegoat. He is given the blame for mankind's loss of Eden—an easy, happy life.*** Thus his story serves to reconcile

---

* Many details below are from the Winnebago version, which Radin presented at length.
** For example, when he carelessly let his penis get chewed to bits, out of the fragments he creates flowers and vegetables for mankind.
*** In the Winnebago Hare version, a paradise in which man could have everything without work is lost because of one of Trickster's misdeeds. He has intercourse with a woman who belongs to a god, the one woman forbidden to him.
Oedipal themes, suggested in this episode, are clearer elsewhere in the Hare version. The Trickster is born of a virgin and has no father. Because of her death,

people to the hardships of human existence and to their creator, who is not held responsible for the Trickster's mischief. The Trickster is also a sacrificial figure; parts of his body and in a sense his whole life are given to mankind.

His career is progressive. After some time the Trickster sees that his misadventures are not simply bad luck. As a result he becomes self-conscious and the process of humanization begins. Eventually he develops a sense of responsibility and goes around doing good deeds although he remains a lonely wanderer. (In becoming a hero he fulfills his destiny, for he had been set on earth to serve mankind.) His life can also be seen as a model of maturation, suggesting that all boys are tricksters until they become responsible men. And it can be interpreted as racial history, going from man's animal origin to his civilized form.

His life is a search for identity, integrity, and sanity. In the beginning he not only lacks feelings, purpose, and knowledge, but his body has no definite form or unity. Its shape and sex are changeable; he carries vital parts of himself (penis and intestines) as detached property in a box; and he treats parts of himself as if they were autonomous. In addition he is unable to make sense of events in his life or of his own behavior.

His life is an ironic commentary on foolishness in human nature and social custom.

There is no taboo he does not violate, no authority he does not challenge. He is an enemy of established order, and therefore an agent of change.

His role is inspirational. The telling of his story is a special, sacred event for the community.

Most of us admire the Trickster secretly; under our conscious and public condemnation of tricksters is identification and admiration. Our enjoyment of picaresque novels and autobiographies includes interest in the heroes of them. As Merton (1957) noted, Americans admire

he is reared by his grandmother. He kills her husband (unintentionally helping mankind by doing so) and later seduces her by trickery.

In Greek myth, the trickster Prometheus (or his brother or alterego Epimetheus) bears responsibility for man's loss of paradise (Brown, 1947). His role is analogous to the biblical Adam's; Pandora (his bride) corresponds to Eve; the trickster Hermes, the phallic god, is Pandora's corrupter, corresponding to the serpent in Eden.

clever knaves. *Even in clinical textbooks the clever tricks of psychopaths are often presented with loving elaboration of detail. Choice exploits are recounted in a manner indicative of wonder and sometimes awe.* (See below and next chapter.) And victims of psychopaths, despite indignation and resentment, sometimes dwell on the details of the tricks used on them. They stress the wit of the scheme and the boldness of the act (Can you imagine it? He even went with me to the bank vice-president and stood next to me when I deposited his worthless check). Thus even when people complain of a psychopath they reveal a fascination in him. Some of them seem to be boasting, as if to say this was no ordinary criminal, as if there were something special in being taken advantage of by a trickster.

If the Trickster is admired in real life as well as in biography, fiction, and myth, then it should be no surprise that we encourage him in our children. When they are small we delight in their impishness, even when we make a sober show of disapproval. We are amused by their errors and clumsiness. And we recount their tricks to friends, sometimes boastfully. As they grow older and the consequences of their mischief grow more serious, our concern does too. But even embittered parents, whose children are in prison after years of trouble, give glimpses of lingering admiration for their tricks. Parents of delinquents as well as of other adolescents begin their complaints in despair or anger only to smile over some of the details. The fascination that the Trickster holds for us would seem to come from our unexpressed desires. The dark hero is closer to our inner selves than the noble one. All of us, beneath our civilized veneer, carry desires to be sensual and free, to eat, indulge in sex or pass air on impulse, to defy authority and to take vengeance on those who slight us. The Trickster does it for us. And in doing so he is our champion, our inspiration, and our scapegoat. His struggle to achieve identity by defying authority is our struggle to the extent that we have become socialized at the expense of our inner selves.

Therefore it seems likely that those psychopaths who have the idea that they are on a mission for mankind, who have the effrontery to suggest that their antisocial behavior has some vague social purpose, may have a basis in reality for those ideas. They may have gotten them from mythology or literature or from knowledge of the veneration accorded knaves in our history. Or they may have perceived that they are expressing what most people yearn to but dare not. More significantly, they may have been reinforced for psychopathic behavior by people who looked to them for hope. This possibility is explored in the next chapter.

THE PSYCHOPATH AS A REDEEMER

As we have been growing more aware of our inner selves, the alienated anti-hero has been replacing the noble hero on the serious stage. Usually he has been an impotent, pathetic figure—a schlemiel.* A newer image in drama is the anti-hero as a figure of power in a bankrupt society. Two recent black plays presented the alienated but powerful criminal as a reformer: Elder's *Ceremonies in Dark Old Men* and Gordones *No Place to Be Somebody.*

In Gordone's (1969) play about the struggle to achieve manhood, a psychopath is the central character. He is in the rackets, is affluent, and moves among weak men who dream of success. He supports them but also mocks and torments them with pranks. The hero has no feelings for women; he is a pimp and uses them as contemptuously as he does men. He is tied to no one.

Gordone's identification of his protagonist with mythic heroes is indicated by his name. The hero, Johnny, is called "J.C." ** When an opportunity occurs to fight an enemy of great power (who is also a menace to the community) Johnny eagerly embraces it; he sacrifices himself in the end.

Sartre (1949) offered a finely detailed dramatic portrait of a psychopath. Hugo, his hero, is also trying to become a man, but he does not even feel that he is a person. In trying to find himself, he has broken with his well-to-do family, married, and joined an underground revolutionary party. Now, at twenty, his situation is no better for these moves. Marriage has intensified his problem because his wife, who is also lost, makes demands on him without helping to define his role. And in the party he is only a marginal member. He identifies with the values and ideals of the party, but his job (editor of an under-

---

* Farce has become an increasingly important dramatic form and modern audiences are moved by ridiculous figures in the plays of Becket, Ionesco, and Friedman. Sometimes audiences have taken anti-heroes more seriously than their creators intended. Stoppard (1967) resurrected Rosencrantz and Guildenstern to be comic figures, but they turned into images of a universal human tragedy.

** And his protégé is called "Gabe." Thus they represent Jesus and God's messenger. In addition, Johnny was born with a veil or caul, which by folk tradition is a relic of Jesus and destines him to be a troublemaker and saint.

ground paper) seems tenuous, lacking in impact. It does not make him feel vital. He craves action, violence.

Overhearing a remark about an assassination plot, Hugo thrusts himself forward for the assassin's role. His fantasy is to place himself next to a prominent person with a bomb in his pocket. "That's the sort of thing I can do," he asserts. His eagerness and insistence are a reflection of how much he hopes to gain. By playing the role of assassin, he will become part of a real drama. He expects to die in the encounter, but it may result in his being talked about, giving him a measure of immortality. Thus he sees the act of assassination as the most significant encounter in his life, one that must have an impact on others as well as on himself. Killing is the one thing he feels capable of taking seriously.

As this suggests, Hugo is estranged from himself, from people, and from life. He has adjusted to his extremely alienated condition by taking things lightly, making a game or joke of everything. Like Gordone's Johnny, he is a trickster. At times he wants desperately to be taken seriously, but he cannot stop playing. He has had to play in order to fill the gaps where he did not know his place or role. Playing has also been useful in softening his misery and in putting people down. He has grown dependent on it and therefore has lost the freedom to stop playing.

Hugo's dilemma of playing versus being, of having to joke when he needs to be taken seriously, is a familiar one. Sartre shows the conflict as an inescapable feature of Hugo's relationship with his wife. Jessica has the same problem with reality and fantasy, the same craving for a real experience and fear of giving up the game. When Hugo tries to explain to her that he is serious about killing someone, she blocks him.

HUGO: Look me in the eyes. No, don't laugh. Listen to me . . . Jessica! I'm serious.
JESSICA: Me too.
HUGO: You are playing at being serious. You told me so yourself.
JESSICA: No. That's what you're doing.
HUGO: You've got to believe me, I beg you.
JESSICA: I'll believe you, when you believe that I'm serious.
HUGO: All right, I believe you.
JESSICA: No. You're playing at believing me.
HUGO: This can go on forever.

Many people have bantering, teasing relationships and know the frustration of pleading for a serious moment while others insist on playing the game. Hugo and Jessica are children for whom the game does not stop. More than most people, they recognize openly that their agreement to play (including playing at being married) is the basic one. Being serious requires mutual consent to suspend the first rule of their relationship. Nevertheless Jessica's amorphous, shifting view of him is what Hugo depends on to confirm his own existence. He tries again.

HUGO: Look at me. Sometimes I tell myself that you only pretend to believe in me and that you really don't, and other times I tell myself that you really believe in me but that you pretend not to. Which is true?

JESSICA: There is no truth.

HUGO: If I could only read your thoughts—

JESSICA: Ask me.

HUGO: What's the use.

A simple plea is not enough. He falls back on what has worked best; *the only way to be taken seriously is to play his part well.* With Jessica, who knows him too well, he never succeeds in becoming convincing or real. And so his intended victim and his assignment become all-important to him. Self-alienation is basic to his character. His search for identity is the motive that brings his destructive and redemptive acts together into an understandable pattern. And his lack of self makes it easy for him to go ahead with his final gamble. He has little to lose.

MONOTONY AND PAIN

In following the psychopath from popular caricature to mythical prototype, the emphasis has been on cultural factors that shaped his image and therefore influenced his behavior. He has been seen in terms of community needs to which he might have been responsive and of cultural models on which he might have patterned himself. Individual or inner determinants of psychopathic behavior have only briefly been considered. In the rest of the chapter an attempt will be made to interpret psychopathic behavior further as a way of dealing with alienation and inner needs.

Bonnie and Clyde and Hugo were not devoid of social instinct, conscience, or anxiety. But there were very important gaps in their emotional life. They and other psychopaths seem to experience monotony, a lack of vividness in their lives, a dead grayness from day to day. Whatever emotions they do feel seem insufficient to give them much of a sense of being alive and involved in life. Psychopaths and other alienated people have something in common with all of us when we are depressed. At such times we do things with little zest, satisfaction, or meaning. Mostly it is the pleasanter emotions that are missing, but sadness too is sometimes absent. It is a common experience to see unhappy-looking people who cannot report any emotion:

QUESTION: What's the matter?
ANSWER: Nothing.
QUESTION: You're crying; you must be feeling something.
ANSWER: I can feel the tears on my cheeks, so I figure that I am sad. But I don't feel different than when I was smiling five minutes ago.

When most other feelings are gone, what often remains is a sense of the unfairness of life with a tone of irritability and impatience. For some it is as if life were in slow motion. But they do not expect anything different in the next reel; they no longer have confidence that today's acts, even if unsatisfying or meaningless in themselves, will lead to something worthwhile tomorrow. Having abandoned the future, they have put their hopes in the present, in kicks. But the present has gone stale and kicks are difficult to come by.

A youth with such a life came to see me under court pressure. The police had picked him up in a street scuffle and found him to be on drugs. He was only seventeen, but in appearance and style he was older. He was tall and heavy, his voice was deep, his tone carried quiet conviction and his words were sophisticated. However he soon revealed that there was nothing in life about which he felt assured. He had dropped out of high school some months earlier after a series of difficulties, impatient about being treated by teachers as a child. During the last year he had been picked up by police a few times for involvement in street disturbances and brought home. Now for the first time he had been arrested, and he had found detention to be a humiliating and nervewracking experience. He hoped I could help him to avoid future detention.

He had already begun to prefer older men, with whom he drank and drove to the shore for long evenings and weekends to "live it up."

After leaving school, he felt further estranged from his peers and stopped associating with them. As he saw it, his town was "dead"; there was nothing to do and people stayed at home and retired early. Boys his age wasted their time hanging out on the street, talking about juvenile, unimportant things. And staying at home made him fidgety and irritable. His main goal was to get a car so that he could go where there was life. Under court instruction, his parents no longer let him use theirs, but he had taken a job since release from detention, and he would soon be able to buy one. The car was a means of getting out of his dull routine to a place where he could feel alive.

He was resentful of his parents for keeping a watchful eye on him. His initial hope that I could help him soon gave way to resentment of me, and he made it plain that he was coming unwillingly and would stop as soon as the court permitted. While in my office, and because he and his parents were paying me money, he felt that he might as well try to use the time constructively, but he had no real hope of a meaningful outcome. For the present, mindful of his probationary status, he avoided drugs and other law violations, but he planned to resume them as soon as the pressure was off.

He was guarded about getting involved personally with me, but had no shyness about the above facts, revealing most of them early. Some of his talk was bravado and some of it seemed like a challenge to me to try to discipline him, but mostly he spoke with resignation. He had given up on education, and, along with it, on having a successful career. Dating was juvenile, and the idea of love or marriage had no meaning to him. He was well aware of his detachment and hopelessness, which he considered a reasonable adjustment to an unfriendly and foolish world. He expected to get into more and more serious encounters with the police; he anticipated that by the time he was in his twenties he would be killed or that he would kill someone, perhaps incidentally while committing a robbery, and go to the electric chair. He saw no other way.

Many who resemble him experience a vague dread connected with the staleness of their lives. The absence of clear feelings is a sign that something is wrong and gives people an uncanny sensation of being not quite alive. "It's terrifying not to feel anything," said a woman having the experience for the first time. But when it is everyday, the terror too is muted, although the situation is actually more desperate. Against this kind of deadness, simple fun is of little help and may well strike a person as childish. The search for kicks may then take more extreme forms; elicitation of pain and risking injury become ways of proving that one is alive and "plugged in."

One need not start out as a masochist in order to turn to pain in the end. Limbo can be worse than hell; emptiness is worst of all. Rosner's (1969) words about depressed people apply here:

> . . . *pain is the only evidence these patients have of feeling anything. "Pain holds me together. If I give up my pain, I have nothing and there is nothing to take its place."*

Joseph, the hero of Bellow's (1944) novel, is expecting to be called for military service. He does not know how long he will have to wait, nor what to do in the meantime. The wait becomes agonizing and disorienting. One day he runs into a friend from the past who refuses to recognize him. Joseph insists, causing a scene. His anger and his loss of control upset him badly, but he feels that the confrontation was necessary. The lack of recognition was a challenge to his sense of existence. He explains:

> *Trouble, like physical pain, makes us actively aware that we are living, and when there is little in the life we lead to hold and draw and stir us, we seek and cherish it, preferring embarrassment or pain to indifference.*

RUSSIAN ROULETTE AND OTHER GAMES

Caught in an unending twilight, "pinch-me," if played ferociously, wakes one up momentarily. One adolescent tried to kill himself because, as he explained, he could not distinguish "the semblance of life and the semblance of death" (Sundberg and Tyler, 1962). But to pinch oneself is not enough. Interaction with other people provides more of a sense of reality than what we do to ourselves. And a pinch of questionable objectivity is not sufficient for one who already is unsure of his own reality and of his ability to distinguish reality from fantasy. In addition, autonomous experiences are self-defeating for one who needs to feel connected; it is more human to have someone else supply the pain—to have a relationship.

We have all seen children, whose more socialized overtures are rebuffed, turn to provoking their parents. We know adults who prefer a quarrel to being ignored. Painful contact is preferred to none at all. Adolescence in our culture is a condition of invisibility, of being tolerated without having status. Many find the amorphous state of being children no longer and not yet admitted to adulthood difficult to endure. A few in high school and more in college turn to desperate measures to clarify their status. A traditional solution which our culture advertises for identity problems is violence. *Red Badge of Courage* and *High Noon* carry the same message as thousands of movies and novels: to become a man, or to prove oneself a man when in doubt, killing with the risk of being killed is recommended. Therefore it should not be surprising if some youths turn to violence for clarification of status and identity.

In seeking release from a condition of dismal unreality through violent contact with another person, a final consideration is unpredictability. The deadened man is like the thirsty lush who closes his eyes and holds his nose: If I see or smell the drink, my mouth will water and dilute it. What he wants is a peak experience. And when he is courting death, unpredictability provides an element of hope that he may yet be rescued.

Therefore driving at sixty in a congested area is preferred to simply hitting oneself. Russian Roulette is preferred to a fully loaded gun. Better still is someone else's hand to pull the trigger. These games put the thrill—which means feeling alive—back into the anticipation of pain. The deadened man arranges for others to hurt him in unpredictable ways.

The last game is suicide. The logic of the final wager is: Only the living can die. In a study of suicidal young black men, Hendin (1969) found that many of them "came alive only through acts or fantasies of violence." Menninger (1938) considered the psychopath a "chronic suicide" along with the drug addict and the accident-prone person:

> In such persons . . . the destructive urge is often of a progressive nature, requiring larger and larger payments until the individual is, as it were, bankrupted and must surrender to actual death.

Courting death also has an indirect payoff: If I do it long enough and hard enough, and escape, there must be somebody up there who loves me. There is a practical side to such logic; Americans come out of their detachment when someone is committing suicide and become interested, devoting considerable effort to save him. Thus there are a number of possibilities in courting death, each of them more hopeful than continuing the gray half-life. There is the ambitious hope which

Jung pointed out of gaining power through death which is not available to the living—supernatural power. There is the limited hope of becoming human in the act of dying. And there is the mixed hope of not dying or of dying only temporarily, and of being saved by Fate, God, or some person who will find one worthwhile and will care enough to furnish a crucial experience which can lead to meaningful rebirth.

Many writers have observed that psychopaths feel half-dead, seek thrills, and court death, but these characteristics have not often been emphasized as basic ones. Bergler (1961) noted that deep depression was hidden beneath the apparent pleasure of many psychopaths and *was manifested when they were not aware of being observed.* Teitelbaum (1965) and Quay (1965) argued that the life style of psychopaths was designed to avert depression and boredom.** Suicidal behavior has often been noted in psychopaths, but interpretations have differed. Cleckley (1964), at one extreme, argued that psychopaths are not suicidal but only pretend to be in order to manipulate people. Robins (1967) went to the opposite extreme, making actual or attempted suicide a criterion for diagnosing psychopaths.*** Between these positions is an increasing body of data showing an exceptionally high rate of deliberate suicide attempts by psychopaths. If we add the indirect and unconscious suicide—the high-speed driving and the game of chicken, the shootout with police, the frequent invitation or provocation to others to assault him, and the wish for or expectation of the electric chair—then we may argue that psychopaths are generally suicidal. At least there are enough suicidal psychopaths to warrant considering theories of suicide to explain psychopathic behavior.

In psychoanalytic theory, suicide is a hostile act. A person may try to kill himself when his situation or character does not allow for a direct attack on the object of his hatred. His expectation that someone close to him will take his suicide as a reproach and will suffer is usually borne out. Thus suicide can be a disguised form of revenge.

---

* The idea that the psychopath smiles for the benefit of the public is discussed in the next chapter.

** McKerracher, Loughnane, and Watson (1968) observed that psychopaths are inclined to mutilate themselves. They do not appear to experience pain or suffering in these acts—on the contrary, they report "wild exultation and excitement." Goodman (1960) saw psychopathic youth as leaning toward violence and death out of a craving for excitement and self-transcendance.

*** See Henderson (1939) and Beall (1969) on suicide as characteristic of psychopaths.

The suggestion above that inviting death can grow out of experiments in pain does not contradict the psychoanalytic theory; a suicidal act can have more than one meaning to the actor. Vengeance and gambling with death will fit together when the hated person is also the one with the power to make the suicidal person feel alive.

Farberow and Shneidman (1961) called suicide a cry for help. Their theory fits well with revenge and gambling in explaining suicide. The theory is that the suicide attempt is not meant to succeed fully —not in extinction. Rather, the goal is help, rebirth, growth. Menninger (1938) remarked on the paradox that "one who has wished to kill himself does not wish to die!" and while he is dying he may plead with the physician to save him. This paradox is familiar to anyone who has lived with a chronic suicide. One woman had made many attempts—more than her husband and children remembered. Usually she turned on the gas not long before someone was due at home, and this timing indicated the interpersonal aspect of her attempts. In time the gruesome experience of entering a house filled with the stench of gas and of reviving her turned the family against her. Coming home meant wondering if they would be in time. Later it came to mean half-hoping that they would be too late. They felt the hostility in her acts, and their growing contempt for her reached the point where they no longer noticed or responded to the pleading aspect of her attempts. In turn, her hostility increased until she did kill herself.

We are not concerned here with suicidal gestures—swallowing aspirin or pricking one's arm at a safe distance from the vein. A suicidal act is Russian roulette with a loaded gun; it means embarking on a course toward probable death. Whatever the underlying motive, the attempt under discussion here is genuine in the sense that one initiates a potentially fatal chain of events and then awaits the outcome. The woman above did not know when one of her family would be home—not as a certainty. There was always the possibility of their being delayed or tarrying deliberately. And, contrarily, a person may hope for rescue even when it is clear that there is little to hope for.

In a study of people who survived serious attempts at suicide, Weiss (1957) found that 15 percent had felt sure of dying and 13 percent had felt sure of surviving. The remaining 72 percent had been uncertain as to what would happen. But almost all of them expected something significant to happen, some change in their lives as a result of the attempt. Weiss interpreted many of these attempts as gambles in which Fate was compelled magically to make the final decision.

The idea of confrontation with death as a gamble is not new. In medieval Europe the angel or figure of Death was conceptualized as a gambler and as an accepter of challenges (Pearson, 1897). When Death came for a human gambler, they were said to roll dice for the man's life.

A person who gambles with his life, seeking rebirth through attempted death, is using a familiar logic. Man has long believed that destruction and growth go together. The image of the phoenix—vigorous renewal out of one's ashes—is seen in many places and forms. The concept of a repetitive life cycle embodies it, as do beliefs in a perpetual harmony in nature. Reincarnation is a fairly direct example of the idea of the unity of death and birth, and such unity is common to a number of Eastern religions and philosophies. Cannibalism exemplifies a similar unity. Jews by tradition receive the name of someone who has died. And the Christian cycle of life, death with purification in fire, and a greater afterlife, was once a powerful example of the idea of renewal. I am not arguing the validity of cyclical concepts of life, but that the idea of trying to come alive by attempting suicide is consistent with traditional views.

Psychopaths usually risk death while engaged in antisocial acts. Therefore we may also consider their antisocial behavior as a possible plea for help. If we do so, we may more easily understand when they clumsily or with seeming indifference invite discovery. Their manner is often provocative. A psychopathic patient, while threatening to smash my office, told me, "Killing someone is the only real way of recognizing him." A few minutes later he cried, "I want to belong, and I'm not part of anything in the world." We have seen incidents in which a child, whose request has been turned down by his mother, attacks his sister or breaks something. The exasperated mother usually condemns his act as scapegoating, which it is, and misses the other message—that he wants something from her but cannot press her further for it in a straightforward way. When a message contains hostility and pleading, it is difficult to respond to both parts. Most of us react more to the hostile part. We do not often accept pleas that come in a destructive form, and we are less likely to accept them from adolescents or adults than from young children.

A problem in interpreting the psychopath's antisocial behavior as a cry for help is that observers are not agreed that he is drawing attention to himself. He is not explicit about wanting attention; he does not openly ask for help, and cryptic pleas to authorities (unsigned notes like "Stop me before I kill again!") are rare. Thus we are left to interpret what is implied in his behavior. The issue is whether his crimes are poorly conceived, making detection easy, or intelligently evasive. Some psychoanalysts have argued that psychopaths seek punishment and reconciliation, and for that reason break the law in crude ways which invite discovery. By contrast, Cleckley (1964) and others have stressed psychopaths' shrewdness, the clever and sometimes brilliant execution of their crimes, and their ability to talk their way out of trouble when caught. The controversy is not one of conflicting data; the same data are interpreted in two ways. For example, the following case was chosen by Rosen and Gregory (1965) specifically to illustrate the charm and deceptive skill of psychopaths. However it lends itself readily to an interpretation of inviting discovery.

A highly intelligent fifteen-year-old boy was being coerced by his father to play in the school orchestra. One day he left his instrument with a local storekeeper and returned home in tears with the story that it had been stolen. He said that a car had pulled up to the curb and a man had gotten out, seized his horn, and driven off.

> *Despite countless past lies, the boy's manner and his tears were so convincing that the father and the rest of the family never thought to disbelieve him. The police were called to talk to the boy and as they were leaving he said, "You know, talking to you has helped me remember what the car looked like—it was green." . . . Again they were taking their leave when the boy began to recall, detail by detail, the make and year of the car, the fact that there were two men in it and the appearance of the men. Finally, he suggested that . . . he might help to apprehend the malefactors by riding around in a squad car with the police.*
>
> *Unbelievably, his offer was accepted, and for several days he was picked up by a police officer after school to cruise the streets of the town for an hour. Periodically, he would shout, "There they go!" and the officer would turn on the siren and force the designated car to the curb. The boy would look at the occupants and shake his head sadly: "No, that's not them—it looked like them from a distance," and the police car would resume cruising. [Boldface added.]*

The burlesque ended when the storekeeper telephoned for someone to pick up the horn.

What is remarkable in this account is not the brilliance of the boy's lies (his story is like many told by much younger and duller children) but the readiness of his family and the police to believe him. In many published cases of psychopaths, as in accounts of confidence tricks, what is striking is the credulity of the victim rather than the credibility of the lies. The remarkable thing about the lies is the complexity of their function.

In the above case, most of the lies were not designed to keep the police at a safe distance. On the contrary, the boy told them in order to prevent the police from losing interest in him. Many policemen would have thought immediately that the boy was trying to involve himself with them. In any case, the persistence of the boy in spending time with the police and the fact that he did not bother to dispose of the horn made the ending virtually inevitable. However, the boy did not force the issue. Whether and when the discovery would occur that would bring his serious need to the attention of authorities was left to Fate.

It is evident that the boy's lies went far beyond his original purpose of getting out of the orchestra,* and that most of them were made up on the spur of the moment. The boy was quick and glib. But he was not really a skillful liar. His story could have been discredited at any time through the storekeeper, and the lies were not really convincing. The fact that his family already knew him to be a liar meant that he had been caught in many lies, not that he had gotten away with them. The fact that the family "never thought to disbelieve" his story about the horn suggests that they wished to believe it.

The same can be said of most anecdotes about psychopaths. Their lies are glib, but they are not carefully constructed and contain easily detectable false details. The cleverness that glitters in their crimes and lies is rarely supported by careful planning. Even when caught, psychopaths do not always bother about preparing and rehearsing an explanation, but often say whatever occurs to them at the moment of interrogation. Glibness, although momentarily impressive, is not convincing in the end. In addition, psychopaths when cornered sometimes tell stories that are so flagrant as to be useless for evasive purposes.

---

* A few other features of the boy's act are noteworthy. First, the detective work in which he engaged with the police was a prank, especially when it came to forcing motorists to the curb. Second, his prank was hostile. Besides the embarrassment caused the motorists, his parents and the police were made fools of. And third, from the low position of being forced to do something he did not want to, he projected himself into a community-service role.

For these reasons the behavior of psychopaths may be construed as indirectly calling attention to themselves and to the fact that something is wrong.

Describing psychopaths as brilliant is usually an exaggeration. When victims go so far as to attribute uncanny intelligence to psychopaths they are exalting themselves as well as the psychopaths. Few people want to advertise the fact that they have senselessly let themselves be taken advantage of. But people who believe that they have participated in an uncanny process seem to derive some exaltation from the experience even if they have lost materially by it.

The idea of the victim being exalted will be discussed in the next chapter, in which the connection between taboo acts, self-sacrifice, and the search for one's place will be explored further and related to formative experiences in childhood.

□   5. THE GAME

When Hugo became an assassin, attempting to transform the lives of people around him, he was unknowingly aspiring to a priestly role. He was offering himself as an intermediary between them and their fate or god. He was also offering his martyrdom. Every hero carries some remnant of the tradition by which kings and priests were considered vicars of god and superior to ordinary people. And martyrs are identified with Jesus and other redeemers in their offer to sacrifice themselves. Martyrdom has a religious function which brings the hero closer to his god.

The psychopath's suicidal acts and his life game of Russian roulette were interpreted in the last chapter as tempting or pressuring a divine power to intervene in his life, to prove that he is loved. Besides the psychopath's dramatic acts, his day-to-day behavior may also be considered an effort to communicate with a deity and establish a position of closeness to one. Such an effort has been seen in the behavior of a special group of psychopathic people whose main occupation in life is a symbolic or ritualized form of communication with Fate. They are called compulsive gamblers, but they fit the traditional criteria for diagnosing psychopaths as well as anyone does. They appear antisocial, callously and selfishly exploitative of people, relatively indifferent about their own welfare as well as others', and so forth down the standard list of psychopathic traits.* The only thing that sets them apart from other psychopaths is their gambling.

But this gambling is a striking activity, unusual in its effects on the public generally as well as on clinicians and scientists, who join in according gamblers a measure of acceptance usually denied to other psychopaths. In discussing gamblers, psychologists, psychiatrists, and sociologists have traditionally emphasized gambling as the important element of the behavior pattern, interpreting it as a sexual and sometimes religious ritual. They have relatively ignored the antisocial acts or treated them as secondary—sometimes as no more than the means which enable the gambler to pursue his intriguing vice. In the analysis that follows, it will be argued that lying and stealing, when engaged in by a gambler, have much the same functional meaning as his betting, and that each of these acts is part of his special role.

It has often been noted that compulsive gamblers lie and steal and pass bad checks when they want to gamble. According to Bergler (1957), all gamblers were psychopathic as children, and lying and cheating are in their character. They do these things psychopathically —that is, easily, ruthlessly, and often without regard for the relatives, friends and acquaintances who are their common victims, and seem supremely self-confident, self-centered, and indifferent to the reactions of others. Their avidity to gamble occupies them to the exclusion of all else. Stories of gamblers who sell home, wife, and children in order to go on playing are based on fact. They treat people as objects to be manipulated.

The reckless, driven gambler, seemingly unable to stop, has been called neurotic or addicted as well as compulsive; no distinctions are implied by the different terms. The driven gambler is the one who concerns us here, although some of the ideas discussed will also apply to those for whom gambling is not so central or powerful a passion. For some at the extreme, gambling means living, and other parts of their lives are as periods of preparation or recuperation between rounds of the main engagement. They may insist that people and relationships are important to them, but they act otherwise when engrossed in gambling. Some plainly state that they feel alive only

---

* Their judgment is notoriously poor, they do not learn from a series of disasters, they are not able to carry out any life plan and they often commit suicide. Family, love, sex, or other interpersonal relationships are minimal or poorly integrated into their lives and they seem to lack emotions. (Their protestations of shame and remorse are not often accepted as genuine.)

when gambling. "The value of life to me is titillation and excitement . . . teetering on the brink. When you are gambling the juices are flowing, you are *really* alive, *really* alive." And without gambling, life is a void (Trippett, 1970, italics in original). Gamblers Anonymous (1964) offered the following statement as typical: "The only place I really felt like I belonged was sitting at the poker table. . . ."

The vital act assumes stranger proportions when we recognize it as a purely symbolic one. As Rosten (1967) said of Hollywood bettors, "The more devoted votaries of the turf place wagers all year round, on horses they do not know, running in places they have never visited, in races they never see." Thus the horses, dice, and wheels have only symbolic value, as do the kings and queens in a deck of cards; they function as pieces in a game, where their relative positions carry assigned meanings that contribute to the passion. The money in the game may seem more like a real consideration, and many insist that they gamble primarily for money. But it is easy to prove that they are mistaken, and psychiatrists, psychologists, sociologists, and anthropologists are largely in agreement: the compulsive gambler is not playing for money. Some say he plays to lose, but the more general, demonstrable fact is that he is using or losing money in order to play. Dostoyevsky spoke for many a gambler when he said, "The main thing is the play itself. I swear that greed for money has nothing to do with it, although Heaven knows I am sorely in need of money" (Freud, 1959).

Bergler (1957) gave a compelling illustration of a gambler's willingness to lose. Riding the train to his therapist's office, the man observed two others playing cards. One was cheating (the patient was sure of it) and won all the other's money. He then invited the patient to play. Although he quite clearly expected to be cheated, the patient felt unable to resist and soon lost all his money.*

The general pattern illustrated in this story has been amply documented. The compulsive gambler typically plays in an unequal game, often a crooked one, where he is the one being fleeced. And his denial of this should not confuse the issue; he has heard the facts and he knows as well as any victim can that the odds are against him. Blanche (1950) went so far as to say, "Most card and dice games are crooked." Although other writers consider this exaggerated, they agree that much cheating occurs.

---

* The mythical gambler "Canada Bill" Jones was warned that the game he was in was crooked. He replied, "Hell, I know it's crooked, but it's the only 'action' in town" (Poinsett, 1965).

Everyone who plays the horses regularly knows two things. The track and the state take a percentage out of the money bet in each race, which is large enough to put the player at a substantial disadvantage to begin with. And trainers enter horses that are not ready to race or instruct jockeys not to press their mounts, with the result that those who know when a horse is ready take money from those who do not know. (If he happens to receive inside information on a race, the compulsive gambler may deliberately disregard it.) Gambling against the house may be a fairer contest. If the casino is an honest one, the player is disadvantaged only by the house percentage. Private games are a greater risk, for the bigger ones are frequented by hustlers and sharps. When the compulsive gambler sits down to play cards, he may not know which of his opponents is likely to cheat him, but he does know that he is exposing himself to be cheated. Penny-ante friendly games may be innocent and offer him a fair chance, but the compulsive gambler looks for bigger sport.

Psychoanalysts have made two main points about gambling. The more widely agreed-on interpretation is that it symbolizes forbidden sex (specifically masturbation and incest), and that losing is punishment for the sin or payment for the pleasure. The second point is that betting represents a series of pleading questions addressed to a goddess (Fate, Fortune, or Lady Luck): Where do I stand? Do you love me? Will you give me a public sign that it is I who am your favorite? Will you be my lover tonight? The thesis presented below incorporates elements of these interpretations around the idea that the compulsive gambler is Jocasta's son, that he is driven to perform for others, and that he has turned from public feats to mysterious rites. He shows the typical features of the hero: abdication of a personal life; feelings of nothingness and purposelessness; readiness to take risks; detachment from others and from values of his culture; and treatment of others and of himself as objects to be manipulated.

SHE LOVES ME, SHE LOVES ME NOT . . .

The superstitious behavior of gamblers is well known. Some of their rituals are deliberately designed to bring luck. Others have only unconscious meanings or are vestiges of long-forgotten practices. Origins of gamblers' rituals have been studied to help explain the meaning of gambling. Practices in primitive societies have been a source for interpretations of vestigial rituals in sophisticated cultures. The following is taken from Levy-Bruhl's (1924) distillation of practices common to a variety of primitive societies.

The methodical preparations of the primitive player are striking. He fasts and may abstain from sex; he purifies himself; he performs special dances; and he tries to dream the right dreams. Immediately in these preliminaries there is a suggestion of a critical encounter—a chieftain preparing for battle, a medicine man for performing his specialty, a youth for sacrifice, or a candidate for an initiation or sacrament.

In many cultures other common activities involve similar rites with similar meanings. Those connected with hunting are more elaborate and suggestive. Sexual abstinence is emphasized before the hunt, and after the kill there are further rituals: "the animal must be appeased, it must be made to accept its death, the [spirit] of the species must be pacified, the hunter must be purified. . . ." The hunter, it seems, despite his elaborate preliminaries, has done something that may offend, making it necessary for him to appease his victim and cleanse himself. The image is reminiscent of a traditional stereotype of sex between unmarried partners in which the male, the aggressor, was expected to court his reluctant partner with elaborate preliminary ceremonies, and afterward, if he were sensitive, to repair the damage to her self-esteem, comfort her, convince her that the act was worthwhile and kiss her. If he were inconsiderate, he might simply bathe (purifying and protecting himself against unfortunate consequences) and leave. If the assignment of sexual meanings to the hunter's acts seems insufficiently warranted, a closer connection is indicated for farmers, who observe similar rituals around planting. Levy-Bruhl noted that in some cultures farmers were still divorcing barren wives to prevent their plantings from being barren.

The rationale for the farmer's and hunter's as well as the gambler's rituals is the belief that success or failure depends upon the attitude of spirits or gods. "It is quite impossible to imagine one can win if these powers do not consent!" (Levy-Bruhl, 1924). Therefore the preparations have the function of conciliating or coercing the deity, of winning consent.*

In preparations for farming and hunting the ultimate goal is per-

---

* The practice of modern contestants in all sorts of sports and ventures of asking divine blessing shows a similar belief. Augustine presented the Catholic view when he said that there is no such thing as chance because God controls everything.

sonal gain, but gambling differs in that material gain is unimportant and the game is competitive. One seeks prosperity by other occupations, but one gambles for a sign that he has been chosen as a divine favorite. The gambler who wins feels superiority, increased power, elation, expansion of his being, and intoxication. He has transcended the "isolation and weakness of his own individuality." He is "conscious of being accepted, protected, saved" by the deity. Losing means the opposite: he experiences depression, prostration, smallness and impoverishment; he is "wounded in the very heart of his being . . . impotent and threatened." The deity has "repulsed him, excluded him, condemned him." He is "reduced to the misery of his own being, without strength and without support."

The habitual primitive gambler seems driven beyond simply seeking acceptance and consent from the deity. That could be done alone, in private communion, and the preliminaries to gambling have that function. But the gambling itself is more ambitious, for the gambler knows that his competitors have also made magical preparations and have also received encouraging private signs (e.g., favorable dreams) before entering the game. The game, then, reduces to a question: Whose side are you on? Not content with private hints, the gambler is forcing the deity to make a public declaration as to who is the chosen one.

The game, as Levy-Bruhl emphasized, is serious, although nonplayers may mistake it for frivolous amusement. The players will often be feeling depressed, desperate, and vulnerable, although they may disguise their feelings by a casual or even light-hearted attitude toward the play. If the public accepts these appearances, the public is misled.

The farmer, hunter, and gambler use similar preparatory rites, which function to make them acceptable or pleasing to a deity, but not for the same reasons. The farmer and hunter have obvious reasons for propitiating a deity, but the habitual gambler's motive is less clear if we accept Levy-Bruhl's statement that material gain is not what moves him. To the extent that the gambler plays again and again, we may infer that the knowledge and exaltation of being chosen do not last and that he requires frequent renewal of proof. Habitual gambling seems therefore to be prompted by a lack of a sense of worth and status. The gambler's idea of himself is so flimsy that he can be crushed by a negative sign. Similarly, a positive sign can mean everything to him.

It would seem, then, that behind habitual gambling in primitive societies is self-alienation and a craving for high status. In addition, the gambler's craving seems to have a sexual component. His preparations suggest the possibility of an amorous rendezvous. Winning makes him feel like a potent man. And he propitiates a different god than the hunter or farmer does. He woos Fortune, who is personified as female in most cultures. And he engages in his ritual pursuit in public. We have seen that a private sign (a favorable dream or other omen) is not sufficient, but merely gives the gambler confidence to press further.

Therefore we may speculate that, in addition to his alienation and poor sense of his own worth, the habitual primitive gambler differs from the nongambler in the following ways: (1) He has a strong need for symbolic love or sex. This suggests that actual love or sex are unobtainable or unacceptable to him, or insufficient. The same is suggested in that, (2) He seeks repeated proof of his potency and no amount of the kind of proof he gets is sufficient for long. (3) The partner whom he courts is also sought by others and must choose between him and them. (4) What he seeks is public rather than private. Thus his craving leads not to the possibility of a satisfying, intimate, and lasting relationship, but to an endless ceremonial pursuit of a disembodied female figure.

If we make the substitution of mother for goddess, these ideas fit together as follows. The gambler's motives are incestuous; his primary sex-love object is unattainable and taboo, and she cannot be sought directly. And his desire and resultant inner conflict are so intense as to hinder him from feeling potent and masculine for long or from finding fulfillment in an actual heterosexual relationship. Thus at least some of his desire for love is alienated; it is experienced in an impersonal, indirect way and its object is a symbol, not a person. He seems to be an alienated person in endless pursuit of a divine female. In these respects the primitive gambler seems to be an Oedipal son with a strong leaning toward ritual and magic.

Many psychoanalysts have compared our sophisticated gambling addict to his primitive counterpart, and it remains for us to see how similar they may be. Beginning with the simplest point of comparison, those who write about today's compulsive gambler emphasize the point that winning, although it excites and gratifies him momentarily, never leaves him satisfied. He does not stop playing after a big win; in fact he seems unable to do so. Many a gambler would dispute that statement, insisting that he will play until his goal of making a "killing" is realized, and then he will stop. Dostoyevsky, for example, and the man described below intended to play only long enough to win the amount needed to repay their debts. But observers find that no "killing" is sufficient. Gamblers do, sometimes, by luck, cleverness, or persistence, win the dreamed-of amount, but they do not then stop. Rather, they proceed to set themselves new, less realizable goals, and to play with greater frenzy and recklessness than before. When they stop, it is because circumstances compel them to (such as when they are broke or when the track closes). Similarly, when they do give up gambling altogether as a way of life, it is usually because they have hit "rock bottom," and are demoralized and helpless, willing to put aside their grandiose ambitions and to humble themselves in front of others, as by joining Gamblers Anonymous.

Hoffman (1968), a compulsive gambler, distinguished the cautious betting, in which he applied his knowledge and often succeeded in increasing his money, from the undisciplined betting of everything at once by which he threw away what he had accumulated when he was on the point of attaining his objective. Behavior of this sort has confirmed the widely held idea that the gambler has an unconscious need to lose or to be punished. He is not content with success. The money, the exhilaration of winning, the proof of his ability, of his having predicted and bet well, and the evidence that Fortune has favored him —these are never enough. Rather than satiating him, rather than giving him the security with which to turn away to activities in which contentment is a possibility, his successes spur him to attempt the impossible. In other words, behind his limited, conscious goals are others which no amount of winning can satisfy. He is a man with an extreme craving.

He wishes for a life that is dramatic, even melodramatic. He longs for the sensation of teetering on the brink of the unknown, for the thrill of being swept upward on the curve of hope, of being cast down the slope of despair (Ludovici, 1962).

Taboo sexual desires have been seen in the gambler's irresistible urge, the exciting activity of his hands, his often-repeated resolutions to quit, the intoxicating pleasure of the game, and the concomitant guilt. Gorer (1967) described the moment of decision—winning or losing—as a climax "frequently accompanied by the increase in heartbeat, involuntary sweating and other vaso-muscular changes which also accompany the act of love." And the increasing tension that precedes the climax is usually experienced as pleasurable.

The jargon of gambling is heavily loaded with sexual references, especially in dice, which is the oldest form. Throwing a desired number is called "coming" and giving a player bad luck is called "putting the horns on." The number four is "Little Dick," and ten is "Big Dick" or "Big Dick, the ladies' man." And a show-off is a "Posing Dick" (Maurer, 1950). Women are excluded from the games by men, or when admitted are not usually treated as feminine; neutral objects of the game, however, take on feminine identity. The numbers 5, 8, and 9 are "Phoebe," "Ada," and "Nina," and a common plea addressed by the eager or frustrated player to the dice or cards is, "Come on, Baby!" or "Be good to me, Honey!" The card queen is called a whore.

The belief in primitive cultures that sexual abstinence promotes success in the game is reflected in our popular saying, "Lucky at cards, unlucky in love." Sex and gambling are considered incompatible; when a habitual gambler is absent from the game, others speculate that he has found a new love, and, conversely, on his return it is thought that his sex life has gone sour. Thus overt sex is emphatically dissociated from the game, but sex symbols abound, which suggests that the game expresses sexual conflict—desire plus taboo.

Particularly significant are the images of courtship in gambling. The objects of the gambler's attentions are Fate, Fortune, or Lady Luck. These goddesses are feminine, and in many cultures Fate or Destiny are conceptualized as being moody, like the stereotype of ordinary women. Thus the crucial factor in dealing with Fate is determining the mood in which she happens to be at the moment (Olmsted, 1962). And the courtship—even in its disguised form—is cautious and conflict-ridden. Fenichel (1945) suggested that the gambler only hints at his plea, that he asks playfully what the answer would be if he put a serious question. In other words, the question is hypothetical and thereby avoids a commitment: If I asked you, what would you say? Ambivalence is also subtly indicated in the well-known gambler's plea, "Luck, be a lady tonight!" The conscious intent is that Luck should be generous and bestow her favors, but the expression "be a lady" implies the opposite. For a female (woman or goddess) to give herself on request has been considered highly unladylike. Rather, to "be a lady" has meant remaining aloof.

If we infer, then, that Fortune is a taboo sex partner, it is not hard to conjecture why. She is a personification of bountiful woman, the provider and bestower of favors, the one who decides when and how much one shall receive—she represents mother.

That gambling represents a strongly taboo act is further indicated by the intense guilt experienced, far out of proportion to the gambling itself, by the willingness to undergo punishment and humiliation (losing, being cheated, and made a fool of), and by the fact that gamblers typically throw away their chances at the point of succeeding. The idea that gambling represents masturbation seems insufficient to explain the amount of guilt and punishment undergone. Even actual masturbation, in itself, should not produce such a reaction, and less so should symbolic masturbation, in itself. On the other hand, the assumption of mother as the forbidden object of the gambler's quest may explain his inordinate drive as well as the guilt, both of which interfere with his leading an ordinary life.

ORACLES AND RITES

Study of primitive cultures and psychoanalysis of modern gamblers indicate that clarification of status is the main motive in gambling. This motive is behind the preliminary ritual of the primitive gambler, which has two purposes: preparatory (making himself fit for the rendezvous); and oracular (obtaining a sign as to the kind of welcome he will receive). With magical-religious aspects less evident in modern society, purification ceremonies have dropped out, although preparations are still seen. Some players consult past-performance charts on horses or stand watching the roulette wheel for some time before making a bet. Others make sure to wear lucky garments, to have lucky fetishes in their pockets, or to enter the track or casino by a particular path.

Oracular preliminaries are much more in evidence. Many seek signs—a lucky feeling, a hunch, a chance remark, event, or dream which is interpreted as favorable—before beginning to play. Obsessive arguing with oneself about whether or not to play is common and can be interpreted as oracular; the gambler seeks in his ruminations the conviction that it is appropriate to try his luck. But, unlike his primitive brother, our compulsive gambler then plays anyway, with or without a favorable sign.

Some gamblers pass a bad check or obtain money by a confidence trick before going to play. Acquiring the money with which to gamble is their conscious motive. But the regularity with which they do it, the risks they take, and other details suggest more complex motives. This behavior is discussed later in more detail; the point here is that check-passing and confidence tricks can be interpreted as preliminary queries. Asking someone to cash a check or believe in a scheme is a way of testing for one's luck or acceptance. If the victim agrees, he is saying that the gambler appeals to him and that he trusts the gambler. When check-passing is done as a preliminary to gambling, we may interpret it as oracular: in asking for money, the gambler is seeking a sign that he can win more significant acceptance in the game.

When the check is bad or the scheme fraudulent, the gambler is asking for something to which he is not entitled, something taboo. If we accept the theory that gambling is a request for forbidden favors, then check-passing is similar. The idea of courtship implies a series of preliminary acceptances before one comes to the question of consummation, and a prudent man looks for signs of encouragement of his preliminary advances before trying to take a woman. It would seem that the sophisticated gambler as well as the primitive one, deeply aware that he is soliciting taboo favors, seeks encouragement in advance of committing himself.

Greenson (1947) suggested that the gambler is saying, "Here is my money, now am I allowed to enjoy certain forbidden pleasures?" Bergler's (1957) patient considered losing natural: "Aren't you supposed to pay for the pleasure?" For gambling to entitle a person to incestuous privileges, he would need to do more than pay for the pleasure and more than engage in ordinary courtship and marriage. What is needed is a special wedding, an initiation more powerful than incest taboos. But gambling is not an initiation; it does not transform the gambler. He does not get to mate with Fortune, but remains preoccupied with preliminaries, stuck in a perpetual courtship.

We may still consider the possibility that gambling is a vestige of a formerly more effective initiation. Indications that the gambler views himself as uniquely chosen and as possessing superhuman powers are abundant. He sees himself as qualified for some unspecified, favored status. Fenichel (1945) emphasized that "the typical gambler consciously or unconsciously believes it is his right to ask for special protection by fate." Bergler (1957) noted the gambler's "supercilious and mysterious smile," and his unbounded faith in his own ability together with deep contempt for other gamblers, whom he sees as "inferior creatures." "I just know I'm going to win. This time I can't lose," he says. Dostoyevsky came to his wife after a series of losses for the last of their money. She reported that he promised unconditionally to win. "He said it *in a tone of complete conviction, as if his winning or not* *winning depended on him alone.*" * Greenson (1947) said, "Many . . . believe concentration will influence the sequence of cards or the roll of the dice." And Bergler (1957) put it more strongly: "When a gambler places his stake on a card . . . he is 'ordering' the next card to win for him. . . ."

To summarize, the primitive gambler and his modern counterpart would seem to have the following in common.

Money is an element in the game, not the object of it:
Money is payment that entitles one to play;
Money adds to the reality of the game, providing the winner with tangible proof that his encounter with the goddess has not been purely imaginary and that he has been favored.
The game, as well as its preliminaries, are essentially ceremonial, with the following functions:
Oracular or questioning, eliciting signs which encourage one to proceed;
Propitiatory or pleading, consisting of a performance and a sacrifice which are pleasing to the deity;
Procural or coercive, consisting of participation in rites that entitle one to forbidden privileges.
The goals of the game are:
Excitement for a person who feels lifeless, hopeless, or cut off;
Incestuous gratification by symbolic intimacy with a goddess who substitutes for mother;
Restoration or recognition of an exclusive, favored position of power.

In addition there is something grandiose and heroic in the gambler's role, and not only in his own mind. The public regards him with some

---

* Quoted with italics in Bergler (1957). Dostoyevsky's megalomanic promise to his wife is so striking that it distracts us from her behavior. She, presumably, was normal; her judgment was not impaired by gambling mania, and she knew of his losing time after time. Nevertheless she accepted his promise, gave him the money, and was disappointed again. Her behavior, thus, was no more realistic than his. And her complicity is typical of that of relatives and friends of gamblers generally. We are struck by the wild schemes and ridiculous promises by which gamblers extract money. We focus our attention on the obsessed gambler, begging, borrowing, conning or stealing money to support his habit. But we tend to forget that his saner associates often go along with him and are in this respect hardly more sensible than he is. It is a fair speculation that they are supporting his habit psychologically as well as with money.

romantic awe and even his psychoanalyst tends to be fascinated by his betting systems.

A MYSTERIOUS MISSION

Alienation was indicated more than it was seen directly in the abstract discussion of gamblers above. In the case material that follows, alienation will be clearer, as will the heroic role of the gambler. Both will be traced to childhood experience. The story of Hoffman (1968) is like many told at meetings of Gamblers Anonymous. The details of his character and life are typical and yet so extreme that he seems like a caricature of a gambler. But that too is typical; exaggeration is a part of the character. Hoffman's autobiography is the most detailed recent document on a compulsive gambler.

Hoffman was a bright, talented, and ambitious man, possessing physical attraction, charm, and a phenomenal ability to impress people. The high point in his life came when he was twenty-nine. Earlier, despite his abilities, he had drifted, taking jobs as they came, doing well in them, and leaving them in an aimless series of adventures. Now, after settling in a new city with his wife and children, he was holding three jobs simultaneously: sales promotion manager for an insurance company, editor of a newspaper, and free-lance advertising copywriter. He produced so impressively that before long he was invited to run for public office. Nevertheless, and despite the fact that he was working a twenty-hour day, he felt that he was not doing enough. Even though others were prepared to proclaim this stranger as a leader of the community, he was dissatisfied with himself and did not feel that he was fulfilling his calling.

It was at this point that he abruptly ran away, becoming a solitary vagrant who only went to people when he needed to cash the bad checks that supported his gambling. When he wrote his story, he had been living much like a derelict, wandering from place to place without baggage or belongings, sleeping anywhere, taking a meal from time to time. He was estranged from his wife and children, and over the years he had estranged himself from everyone he had known in his life. His ideals as well as his possessions had been left behind except for his intense but unfocused ambition. He felt less clear than ever about how to live and about the meaning of relationships with people. He was wandering in search of himself. Of the period since leaving his family he said, "I had embarked on a journey I had not wanted to take, fancying myself rather more an interested observer of the trip and its outcome than the sole traveler. . . ." In a state of misery, guilt-ridden, often denying himself food, lodging, and clothes, he nevertheless felt closer to his vaguely sensed special vocation. He compared his desperate journey to a Marine Corps expedition: "my mission and theirs were similar, both requiring courage and sacrifice, both unpleasant but necessary tasks."

This briefly noted theme of dedication is almost lost in his detailed description of the more usual features of a gambler's life: his psychopathic opportunism; his recklessness and grandiosity mixed with self-hatred and depression; his abortive, self-defeating pattern of life; and his testing and humiliating of those who offered him friendship. Also typical, but clearer than in most gamblers, is Hoffman's detachment from himself:

> *I was aware that I always thought about myself in the second person. . . . I thought of my criminal self as someone else. My real self, I thought, was looking on, interested in the outcome, but not particpating in the contest.*

Hoffman had been a precocious child and a talented and productive young man, showing when very young a strong desire for success and fame. His only clear goal had been to become a successful athlete. When he failed to win recognition in that area, he began to drift: "I did not know what I could be or what I wanted to be." He left college and wandered from job to job, taking whatever came his way, becoming increasingly detached from himself and others. After he left his wife and children to devote himself to gambling, people became largely objects to him to be manipulated for his momentary use.

Yet what he hoped for was not simply selfish. When winning, he sometimes sent money to his family, but he denied himself; his only material indulgence was alcohol. Winning or losing, he gave waitresses big tips, gave money and advice to strangers, and lied to impress people that he was doing well. Impressing others was always a matter of priority. Even his autobiography, despite his conscious intention to humble himself publicly as is done in Gamblers Anonymous, consists of a long boast. He displays his knowledge of various games and he dwells on his ability to pick horses. (Of his superior gambling skill he has no doubt, and he attributes his losses to the intervention of God against him.) He shows his phenomenal memory: his mental file on horses' records; his recapitulation of the names of those on which he bet, the amounts of his bets, and the payoff prices. He boasts of his work ability: his quickness in mastering skills and situations, and his capacity to work very long hours at remarkable levels of productivity.

His biggest boast is about his ability to "con" people, and a large part of his book is a recital—with names and amounts—of his adventures in passing bad checks. His success in exploiting people sometimes seems astonishing. For example, time after time he approached a stranger or old acquaintance in the crumpled, dirty clothes in which he had slept, unshaven, fatigued, poorly nourished, and empty-handed —looking the part of a bum—and convinced the man that he was a prosperous executive or professional momentarily without cash. He tried his trick with some success even on people who had been warned about him.

Of his superior intellect and the knowledge acquired in college he made little use; he was a performer of tricks. And, because people generally are skeptical about a stranger who asks for money, Hoffman was like a magician working in front of a doubting audience which was alerted to the possibility of his using tricks and deception to gain his effects. His special skill was impressing and manipulating people, getting them to believe in him, and he spent much of his time doing it.

It is easy to exaggerate Hoffman's manipulative skill and to ignore the willingness of his victims to be exploited. The role of victim, despite protestations to the contrary, implies conscious or unconscious readiness to be deceived and the wish for an illusion. A magician's audience shows in the extreme the ambivalent role of audiences generally: skepticism with awareness that deception is being practiced, that stage skills are being employed; and simultaneously the wish that the trick be done well so that the illusion is convincing and transports one beyond routine reality. Whoever wants to be inspired must be prepared, like any audience, to suspend disbelief.

The elements of Hoffman's art, when exposed to view, seem insufficient to explain their effectiveness. There is Hoffman's handsomeness, although he does nothing to enhance it. There is his style of boyish candor and enthusiasm, but he lacks patience and thoroughness, often inventing his story as he goes along, sprinkling it with clues which could be used to discredit him, planting absurdities which must be ignored if the illusion is to be maintained. He is glib, a facile if compulsive liar. Probably more important is his perseverance and the reckless intensity with which he plays his part, for many times we see a hesitant victim won over by Hoffman's insistence, backing off from a confrontation, from a decisive test of the illusion. (When he met resistance, Hoffman pressed the victim to yield or to call his bluff, with the prospect of jail. He even passed checks on policemen.) Perhaps it was Hoffman's commitment to his role that was the key element. He was a performer and he played out of habit, whether or not there was a cash audience present. He did not stop lying and promising; he gave away illusions for nothing. And when he asked for money (usually twenty-five dollars or a hundred), he was often surprised to learn that he could have gotten much more.

An audience suspends disbelief in the presence of an actor who throws himself into his role. If that role is a significant one, touching fundamental emotions, the audience is supposed to be transformed by the performance. And the more it has been disappointed, the more cynical and lacking in faith the audience has grown, the more it craves a convincing actor, the more it needs an illusion.

In stressing money as the goal of his confidence game, Hoffman was missing something important in his relationship with his victims. That he needed money was true but not clearly relevant; he was easily capable of getting much more by other methods, and he willingly performed for free. There was, of course, hostility in his exploitation of people, but that too seems limited and insufficient to explain the endless repetition of his confidence trick for relatively small amounts of money. It seems more likely that his performance had a ritual function and that the money served as proof that his behavior was accepted and approved. Hoffman was doing what his life had prepared him to do, and his act was in demand; these seem the key elements in the success of his confidence trick.

Besides passing checks, Hoffman liberally dispensed promises wherever he went, to strangers as well as those who knew him. He offered to perform wonders: to win; to show others how to win; to do complex jobs for which he had no experience; and to work astonishingly long and hard without consideration of his own feelings or needs. And he was able surprisingly often to do these things for a time, although in the long run those who accepted his promises were disappointed.

Most of Hoffman's promises were trivial (like offers to visit people) and given without asking anything in return. Many of his promises were genuine in that he intended to carry them out. They may have served to raise his self-esteem. However, many other promises were knowingly false, and because they served no apparent purpose of his own we may look for their meaning in their effects on his audience. People were impressed by them, entertained, comforted, reassured, and even inspired to efforts on their own behalf. The most general effects were to elevate the spirits of the hearer and to inspire his faith in Hoffman.

If we add Hoffman's confidence tricks, promises, boasts, pretenses of success and affluence, and his generosity with money, advice, and instruction, we see that he spent much of his time inspiring people. This inspirational function seems basic in defining his role and in explaining people's acceptance of it. *People were exploiting him at the same time that he exploited them.*

The above discussion applies to Hoffman's preliminary behavior. He then went and gambled, sometimes winning for a time, but ending each sequence by losing everything. While losing, he stayed in character, pretending to those around him that he was winning; he smiled, continuing to help them and denying needs or problems of his own.

In addition to the above, Hoffman's story shows a number of features which, although common, are less obvious in the lives of most gamblers.

Hoffman often thought of himself as a loser, although he never stopped trying to convince others that he was a winner.

Hoffman saw himself as involved in a continuing struggle with a hostile deity.

His desire to hurt and humiliate his family, indicated in a variety of indirect ways early in his odyssey, became conscious and deliberate toward the end. Early, before he was conscious of his malice and despite his express concern to protect his family, he passed checks on his hometown bank, with the result that police and others harassed and embarrassed his wife. Similarly, when he spoke of his fear that his father might be hurt or killed by the knowledge of his son's gambling and check-passing, we have reason in the details of their relationship to infer that Hoffman's fantasy revealed a wish for revenge on his father.

Hoffman's detachment from himself is clearly marked: his lack of a sense of identity and goals is stated, and his confusion about his own emotions and desires is indicated in his use of clichés which hardly serve to hide the fact that he is describing his feelings incorrectly. For example, he describes the "love" between himself and his wife in storybook terms after it is reasonably evident that both of them prefer to be apart.

Not many gamblers have spoken of their gambling careers as constituting selfless missions, although many share with Hoffman a consciousness of being uniquely chosen, supernaturally sponsored, and of leading a life which is charmed as well as damned.

In focusing above on Hoffman's gambling, lying, and check-passing, a substantial but less dramatic part of his narrative has been omitted in which he recounted some of his ruminations. Not having accepted his own behavior, Hoffman usually wrestled with himself—sometimes for hours—before coming to a decision to pass a check or to go to the racetrack. In these ruminations about adopting a course of action and about his own moral status, the stereotyped quality of his thinking is apparent. The moral injunctions with which he fought his impulses and the rationalizations for indulging himself were endlessly repetitive, trivial, and indecisive. Thus these ruminations were clearly compulsive and may be considered a preliminary ritual. And if we accept the idea that Hoffman's lying, check-passing, and gambling as well as his rumination were ritualistic, we come to the conclusion that the bulk of Hoffman's time was spent in ritual.

Hoffman's life journey began in a small Midwestern town, where he was the last child but the only son born of a rather unhappy marriage. His mother was forty-nine at his birth, his father fifty-five, and his four sisters already grown and gone from the home. Hoffman's father, for whom he was named, was a high school athletic coach, a fanatic about his work and a phenomenal success at it. However, he had not reached beyond this limited glory—he had refused a call to coach at Notre Dame, among others. Similarly, he had shown considerable scholarly promise and success with a couple of books, but then had aborted his career as a historian. In his middle years, when not busy with his coaching, he preferred walking, fishing, and hunting to being involved in the home. He evidently had already detached himself from his wife; to his son he was aloof, untouchable, inaccessible. No interest, no feeling whatever toward his son is indicated in the book, even though Hoffman idealizes his father. Hoffman's mother, "a dreary, spiteful woman" whose life had been going downhill for sometime, had grown to hate her husband. She evidently had expected much of this talented man and gotten rather little, living an embittered, lonely life.

The preconditions for Jocasta mothering were present in the situation: an aged woman, long unproductive in her own life, frustrated by a potentially capable but unwilling and distant husband, resentful and depressed, and thrown together alone with her only son. Too few details of the boy's childhood are given to know if she did, in fact, fasten on him intensely when he was born, but it is clear that she did so before long. She transferred enormous expectations onto him. Although he grew into a highly intelligent, charming, and attractive youth who tried hard to please her and says that he disobeyed her for the first time only when in college, she reminded him over and over that he was a great disappointment to her. When he slipped, no matter how slightly, she ridiculed him, and when he was ten, because of a minor lapse of his, she stopped speaking to him. Thus her enormous demands upon him are clearly enough indicated, as is her rejection of him. What is not shown is that she loved him or indulged him. Hoffman reports the contrary; he sees her as a purely hateful creature, and he makes his hatred of her plain.

There are, however, a few reasons for questioning Hoffman's characterization of his mother as entirely negative toward him. His pictures of both parents are obviously exaggerated and unidimensional: the father comes across as saintly, as being devoted to a legion of boys (but never to Hoffman, who nevertheless insists that he admired his father and denies any hostile feelings toward him). For Hoffman to have grown into so ambitious and proficient a youth implies that someone took considerable interest in him and in his performance. And the details of their relationship as well as the fact that she was the only one involved with him make it clear that it was his mother. It was she who expected things from him and who deceived, manipulated, threatened, coerced, and ridiculed him continually, trying to shape his behavior. It was she who was so often disappointed in him. And it was she to whom Hoffman responded and whom he tried to satisfy until he was in his early twenties.

As he broke from her, he courted and married a goddess—a woman whom he describes as a striking beauty, talented, intelligent, saintly in her virtues, and something of a star performer herself. But he came to hate her and tried to destroy her, turning from her to pursue Lady Luck.

The above argument is not meant to suggest that a wholesome, loving relationship existed between Hoffman and his mother, but that along with their mutual hatred was an intense attachment. In view of his mother's investment in him and her expectations of him, it is not surprising that Hoffman developed precociously. By the age of six he had written a lengthy short story and performed astonishing feats of memory. And in view of the exclusiveness of their relationship it is no surprise that at six he was already obsessed with guilt and developing the sexual inhibition and abstinence that persisted in his adult life. The details of his family life imply that his mother (and not the nuns whom he blames) was the source of his great guilt and sexual inhibition.

Hoffman's story shows him as an Oedipal son and his mother as Jocasta. He transferred his efforts to please from his mother to his wife and then from his wife to Lady Luck. The goddess whom he pursued seems to have symbolized his ambivalent mother, who was both fanatically interested in him and angrily rejecting.

In turning to the question of how common Jocasta mothering is in lives of compulsive gamblers, the main problem is that writers have neither looked for it nor reported on it. However, the details of mother-child relationships which have been reported for gamblers are generally consistent with Jocasta mothering.

THE GAMBLER AND HIS LOVE

After Hoffman's, the biographical account of gambling with the most relevant details of parent-child relationships is Richardson's (1967). Richardson suggested that his mother started him toward gambling by giving him a toy roulette wheel when he was a child. The connection is not entirely trivial. Although he commented only briefly on his early experiences, a clear enough picture of double Jocasta mothering was sketched. He was an only child, raised in a household consisting of himself and two women—his mother and maternal grandmother. His father, described as a small, gentle, unmanly person, had been separated from the family by divorce. Another and especially significant absent man was his maternal grandfather. A profligate gambler, a man who had "lived a life of complete license and self-indulgence," and had abandoned his wife and daughter, he was still adored by these women as a hero. The grandmother expected Richardson to be like her husband.

The mother also had high expectations of Richardson and an

extravagant view of his abilities. She was "always urging me to do outlandish things. . . ." Richardson referred, without being more explicit, to his mother wanting him to have sexual exploits as a child. He grew up with the idea of triumphing in everything he did. However, when he turned to gambling in later years, it was after a series of personal and professional failures.

When he began to learn about gambling, he found it "Eden-like" and as providing through divine intervention "the answer to what all men want to know; namely, which of us are the elect. . . ." Receiving an advance to write a book on gambling—more money than he had ever had in his life—he felt tempted over and over to stake it all on one blind bet. "I want to know, I want finally to know . . . whether or not I am to have any kind of grace in this life." In toying with this idea, in anticipating doing it, he "would dress slowly and impeccably, as though preparing for an elaborate formal ritual." The description is reminiscent of the preliminary rites of Levy-Bruhl's (1924) primitive gamblers.

The picture of his mother as Jocasta is clear enough: a woman who idolizes her lost father and has little interest in her lowly husband, seeking realization of her dreams in her son. The unfolding of Richardson's need to excel and his growing detachment from himself and others, as he gives up on his marriage and on love affairs to "pledge loyalty to Fortuna" are shown. And in his courtship of the goddess through gambling, the ritual character of his preparations and the oracular aspect of his betting are clear. He leaves us to draw the connection between the goddess and his mother, giving ample evidence of a close attachment to the latter.

Galdston (1967) titled his paper "The Gambler and His Love," and implied that the gambler's love was mother. In the exemplary case he cited, because of parental separation, the boy had an exclusive relationship with his mother until he was seven, when she sent him out to be apprenticed, which resulted in his losing her and becoming homeless. As an adult he came to Galdston for help with feelings of depersonalization. He felt remote from his wife and from the many prostitutes and pickups whom he sought out, and was not, in fact, close to anyone. In his middle years he met a woman who pursued him with unfailing devotion and demanded nothing but love from him. Upset by her and always suspicious of her intentions, he nevertheless became emotionally involved. The year-and-a-half of their relationship was the only period in his adult life when he did not bet, illustrating the proverbial substitutability of love and gambling.*

There is one systematic study of a large group of gamblers which focused on mother-child relationships; it strongly implicates Jocasta mothering as a cause of gambling. On the basis of interviews, Olmsted (1962) reconstructed a typical family pattern for gamblers as follows. The mother was hungry for love and sex, not getting much from her husband, not satisfied with what she did get, or in many cases not having a husband. She was so greedy for affection from her son that he learned to suppress his own desires and to simulate emotions that pleased her. As a result he became superficially charming and amiable, an expert at amusing and flattering people with lies and lightly given promises. He went out of his way to please, and the public accepted him for his charm. On the other hand, these same qualities created a serious handicap to the formation of enduring relationships.

His mother's need for affection led also to sexual complications:

> . . . it often comes out that the mother kept the child sleeping in her room until he was ten, eleven, twelve, that there was considerable physical contact, with hugging and kissing and so forth, that she engaged in behavior with him that would be described as flirting in any other context.

While overstimulating her son sexually, she discouraged visible sexual activity, with the result that he masturbated much, became severely inhibited with women, and often had potency problems.

This mother spoiled her child, but not happily or freely. Rather, she emphasized over and over that she was a martyr and that he was a disappointment to her. And her indulgence was erratic. For example, she sometimes fed her baby before he had time to feel hungry, but at other times ignored his cries for food. The son was unable to discover consistent patterns in his mother's behavior; he could not learn how to deal with her in order to obtain regular gratification. Whatever he tried seemed to work sometimes and to be ignored or punished at other times. His life was "subject to good days when everything you do is right and cannot fail and bad days when you cannot succeed no matter what you do." The key to the world seemed to depend on the

---

* Greenson (1947) also noted that gambling and mother-love are substitutable. For other cases with Oedipal data see Harris (1964), Geha (1970), and especially Lindner (1950).

mood of his mother, and she had many more bad days than most mothers. Her mood was his luck, and he came to see the world as a game ruled by a motherlike Fate.

In addition, her wishes became his, and he failed to develop autonomous identity and adequate responsiveness to his own feelings. And in developing a concept of masculine identity, he did not pattern himself on any real man, but on the idealized concept of a man which existed in her fantasy.

The situation of mother and son seems to have been one of constant sexual frustration, inasmuch as her incestuous inhibitions prevented her from gratifying him overtly and from accepting gratification openly from him. Her solution, according to Olmsted, involved an exchange of symbolic gratification which became the basis for his interest in games with sexual symbolism.

Olmsted's reconstruction of formative experiences provides a basis for explaining the main characteristics of gamblers. The pattern described seems particularly likely to produce a tendency to perform for others. This fits with the observation that the gambler is often a performer in some other activity: a traveling salesman (Olmsted, 1962; Gamblers Anonymous, 1964), an athlete (Trippett, 1970), or an entertainer (Rosten, 1967).

If we ask whether psychopaths who are not gamblers are also Jocasta's sons, the answer is less clear. Early studies of psychopaths indicated the opposite; parental neglect rather than interest was the usual finding (e.g., Levy, 1951). Later research has been contradictory, pointing to a variety of family situations. Most researchers have not been looking for Jocasta mothering and the following selection of studies is not typical. However, it is suggestive.

Greenacre (1945, 1952) abstracted a "typical family" of the psychopath from many of her cases; it resembles Olmsted's picture of the gambler's family. The father is a remote and critical person, feared by the son; he is respected outside the home but held in contempt by his wife. The mother is an attractive, pleasure-loving woman. She indulges her son and forms an intense narcissistic attachment to him, treating him as a part or manifestation of herself.

As a consequence the son develops an exhibitionistic orientation; he performs for the glory of his parents (his mother particularly). He is under great pressure from them not to fail. When he does, his mother covers up for him, denying his failure. Under the combination of pressure and special protection, he develops a wanton streak, a "total practical disregard of consequences. . . . He behaves as though . . . consequences were meant for the other man, but not for him; as though he will in some way be exempt, or will be miraculously saved" (Greenacre, 1952).

While the mother is making heavy demands on her son, what she gives to him is inconsistent according to Greenacre (1947). The child sees no pattern; his gratifications seem to come according to parental whim, which he later conceptualizes as divine intervention or luck. And he finds only one way of enhancing his chances of gratification— pleasing his mother. As a result, his orientation to life is based on ingratiating himself and on developing magical ways of promoting good luck, with willingness to take chances. Work, for example, seems irrelevant to satisfaction in life. Greenacre was struck by the psychopath's reliance on "the magic of talk" to accomplish his ends, and his confusion of symbolic gestures with actual deeds.*

Outwardly, psychopaths live for the moment, seeking thrills or wins, but these experiences seem to serve unconsciously as tokens of a greater reward to come—of renewal of a favored relationship with a deity and return to paradise. The token aspects of their encounters are carried to an extreme by the compulsive gamblers among them, whose main occupation is entirely symbolic in its significance. The gambler's ritual in modern society retains the religious function seen in primitive cultures insofar as it is proprietiatory, sacrificial, sacramental, oracular, and inspirational. These aspects are also present although less apparent in psychopathic behavior generally—in the lying, confidence tricks, and various methods of courting death.

---

* Heaver (1943) abstracted a similar family picture from a group of hospitalized psychopaths. For related findings see Gilbert (1948), Hare (1970), Szurek (1942), Johnson and Szurek (1952), Reiner and Kaufman (1959), and Winnicott (1958).

6. OEDIPUS IN AMERICA

Gamblers in Africa sometimes bet themselves into slavery. When they had gambled away their wealth, they offered themselves; if they lost, their freedom was forfeited. In America, Indian gamblers used to wager their liberty, and today's compulsive gamblers do it too, although in less obvious ways. Those who pass checks, steal, or embezzle funds in order to play are risking imprisonment. That risk is striking when it is unnecessary, when money could be obtained safely, as is usually the case. Richardson, in choosing to "pledge loyalty to Fortuna," was consciously submitting himself to a tyrant, as do all gamblers. The act of submission is also seen in psychopaths who offer their lives. Athletes offer their bodies, but often lose their identity.

Characters in fiction who sold their souls to the Devil felt they were giving up something of value. But when modern man sells the equivalent of his soul—his life, freedom, or identity—he seems to feel that he has little to lose. He may already be one of those described by Fromm (1955) "who acts and feels like an automaton; who never experiences anything which is really his. . . ."

To men who feel they are losing little when they lose themselves, but retain the restless seed of ambition, the appeal of becoming a hero is likely to be intoxicating. As Thucydides said of Athenians, such people "are adventurous beyond their power and daring beyond their judgment. . . ." Concepts like duty, patriotism, honor, success, and victory need no explanation for them. When the call is couched in these terms, many answer it. We had difficulty a few decades ago in understanding the willingness of Germans to give up liberty and life in following a dream of superiority. But that was their dream. Ours needs little justification. We consider our ascendancy in space as well as on earth our manifest destiny. The more ambitious the goal, the more appealing it will be to a gambler.

> . . . sometimes a wild idea takes such firm hold upon one's imag- ination and feelings that, impossible and absurd though it be, one accepts it at last as having the stamp of feasibility and reason. Not only that, but if one's wishes, one's strong desires, happen to coincide with the idea, one recognizes the latter as something fore- ordained, fated—inevitable (Dostoyevsky, quoted in Bergler, 1957).

When such fantasies take hold in a nation, the only people whose ideas sound strange are those who argue that it may be just as well to be a second- or third-class power.

The call to glory stirs most of us. The appeal of Fortune would seem to be rooted in unconscious experiences from our formative years —experiences with the first goddess, the one who gave, withheld, and promised. All our mothers were important in our lives, but not all of them are represented in our dreams as sensuous, magnetic goddesses. Those who had such an impact were not necessarily radiant beauties; many were aging, bitter women. The main thing about them seems to have been their interest and devotion in their chosen sons. The ex- clusiveness of the relationship—more specifically, the lack of alterna- tive people to whom the infant could turn—gave the mother great power over him. In the circumstances described, she was virtually the only one from whom he could get sustenance, comfort, or pleasure.

Many mothers have such power; their numbers have been increas- ing with the decline in family size and the absence of aunts and grand- mothers in the home.* The modern Jocasta seems most likely to be found in middle-class families. Upper-class mothers are less tied to domestic life by convention and situation. They feel freer to devote themselves to outside activities and specifically to be away from their

---

* A trend in the opposite direction may emerge from increased use of day care and nursery school for small children, communal living, and women's liberation generally.

children. And their attachments to their children have limited impact because of governesses and other domestics who play a part in the rearing of upper-class children. The situation of lower-class women is also less conducive to forming close attachments to children; more than their middle-class counterparts, poor women hold outside jobs and make use of day-care facilities for toddlers. And they are more likely to be living with parents or in-laws who share in child care. Thus Jocasta mothering, while not limited to any class, would seem to be especially likely in the middle class (see Green, 1946).

The mythical hero was usually a first or only child, and the same is true of his actual counterpart. For example, first and only children predominated among astronauts and fighter pilot aces (Forer, 1969). Systematic studies of birth order show heroic personality traits to be typical of first and only children. Forer reported that first-born sons (more than later ones) felt alone, lacked interest in personal relationships, acted self-confident (although they were particularly troubled by fears and feelings of inadequacy), showed achievement orientation, attended college, and became eminent. In addition, relationships to authority played a great role in their adult lives. More than later children, they were conformists or rebels, or both in alternation. And when volunteers were asked for, first sons offered themselves. Toman (1969) found that first sons were the ones who inspired and led people, sought to dominate other men by force or cunning, and accepted situations of extreme hardship.

A first child is an only one during the earliest years of his life, and therefore first and only children are the most similar in character. Forer reported that only sons, like first ones, were inclined to please and manipulate people, to be courageous, and to be particularly troubled by Oedipal problems.

Parental behavior which fosters distinctive personality development in first and only children has not been dealt with in depth. However, superficial observations are suggestive in relation to the concept of Jocasta mothering. It is the first child (more than later ones) whose birth is a terrifying and miraculous experience to his mother. And it is he who is expected to be capable and who is given responsibilities. Forer noted that he is the object of the highest parental hopes and efforts to make him into a paragon. In addition, it is the first child whose arrival usually leads to abandonment of a woman's education or career. And when a woman feels trapped at home or in an undesirable marriage by motherhood, it is usually her first child whom she identifies as the cause of her predicament. The more profound her regret and despair are, the greater are the consequences for this child. Thus he would seem the likely candidate for a sacrificial, heroic role.

To summarize, although the Oedipal son is found in all birth positions and economic classes, he seems most likely to be the first or only child in a middle-class family. The very social conditions which maximize frustrated ambition, loneliness, and despair in mothers also concentrate in their hands power over their children. The way they use the power seems critical to the development of alienation in their children. Mothers identified in earlier chapters used it to produce heroes. They exerted their influence on emerging behavior in highly selective ways, although not always deliberately. As Olmsted (1962) said, they used it to get their sons to suppress their own impulses and to satisfy the desires of the mothers. The following account illustrates how a mother can be selective unconsciously; it is a model for producing alienation from self. This mother and her half-year-old child were under detailed observation for many months (Brodey, 1959).

> As I watched Mrs. Crompton play with her infant boy, I noted that she was aware only of movements in the child that she herself had "initiated"—if the child smiled in response to his mother's smile, the mother responded. If he smiled of his own accord, Mrs. Crompton, though desperately clinging to the child's every move, was entirely unresponsive, and, it seemed, unaware. The child's autonomous smile did not seem to exist for her in any way. It did not alter even the timing of Mrs. Crompton's frantic efforts to have the child smile. . . .
>
> Mrs. Crompton did not, at any time while observed, acknowledge the child's lead.

And she prevented him from having a relationship with anyone but herself. Brodey inferred that under the conditions described an infant learns that maintenance of the critical relationship in his life depends on his behavior conforming in content and timing entirely to his mother's projected expectation. In other words, he is conditioned to behave in response to the fluctuations of her attention, mood, and interests, and to those of his own which mirror hers, rather than to those of his own which are autonomous.

If such a mother were virtually the only source of reward and punishment in a baby's life, he would learn to smile when his mother expected him to. Rosenthal and Jacobson (1968) documented the extent to which a person's behavior can be influenced by his mentor's unvoiced expectations. The invisible thread which links the subject to those expectations would seem to be the selective attention of the mentor. Like Mrs. Crompton, we all tend to notice things we are looking for and to miss things that do not interest us. And we can only reward what we notice. By limiting our attention in a child's behavior to those acts which we expect, we will be conditioning him to become sensitive to our cues and to ignore his own.

IDENTITY AND ALIENATION

The self-alienated performer is not new in psychology. There are a number of graphic descriptions of him,* but they have had little impact on the mainstream of psychological theory. Winnicott (1965) offered a few simple hypotheses relating alienated behavior to mother-child interaction. The following is an adaptation of his ideas; it will be used as a base for commenting on child-rearing practices and other aspects of culture as they affect alienation.

1. *Responding to an infant's needs promotes the development of true self in him.* Responding means indulging his needs or at least trying to: feeding him when he is hungry with food that suits his taste, comforting him when he is in distress, and playing with him when he wants to play. Indulging an infant's needs has the effect of validating them, reinforcing them as a basis for his behavior. Having a well-developed true self corresponds approximately to being natural, spontaneous, genuine, self-actualizing, or authentic.

2. *Compliance by an infant with needs other than his own promotes false self.* False self refers to behavior that is socially appropriate without reflecting individual desires or aversions. A person who eats because food is offered him without regard to his hunger or whether he likes the food is manifesting false self. External stimuli or demands need not be inconsistent with one's own inclinations. And when they are, one's selfish interests may be served by ignoring one's inclinations.

---

* See the "role player" (Goodman, 1960), the "as-if" personality (Deutsch, 1965), the "marketing" personality (Fromm, 1955), and the "false self" (Winnicott, 1965). Laing's elaboration of the concept of false self in a number of well-received books (e.g., Laing, 1965) remains outside the mainstream of psychology.

We have all experienced threatening situations in which our welfare depended on maximal attentiveness and acquiescence to external demands. But hopefully we retained the ability to distinguish such situations from less threatening ones. False self is extreme in people who no longer discriminate, but habitually respond to others' expectations.

True and false self are defined independently of each other. By definition, one could exist with or without the other, although in reality both are always present. Concepts of true and false self have been much simplified here and distinctions between them exaggerated for convenience of presentation. In reality considerable blending of true and false self would occur in most people, although separation between selves is a mark of alienation. Applying the distinction between true and false self to patterns of mothering, it follows that a mother who ignored her infant would not be fostering true or false self. The mothers described in this book, out of their fondness and interest in their children, would be fostering true self. However, because of the heavy demands they make on the children, they would be fostering much false self.

All of us grow up with a mixture of indulgence and demands, with our behavior a composite of spontaneity and social facade. True self does not refer only to inborn drives, like hunger and sex, and true self is not inborn. It develops largely out of a child's experiences and is composed of a multitude of inclinations (needs, interests, tastes, fancies, bodily sensations) and of ways of expressing and implementing them. A newborn shows only inborn inclinations, but by the time he is a few years old most of his inclinations are acquired ones. False self is not false simply to one's biological impulses; it is also—and most importantly from a psychological viewpoint—false or unresponsive to most of the self that is derived from social experience.

According to Winnicott, false self is troublesome when it is mistaken for true self. Such confusion is fostered when a parent acts in a way that treats the false as true or the true as false. For example, a mother may identify her child as "my Billy" when he complies with her needs. And when he expresses his own she may say, "That's not my Billy. You didn't really mean that. Did you learn that from the boys in the street?" If the boy acquiesces to such identification of his behavior, his false self will become publicly identified as the true one. According to Winnicott (1965), "When the false self becomes exploited and treated as real there is a growing sense in the individual of futility and despair." And when the individual himself makes this misidentification, taking his social facade for his true self, he may feel so desperate as to try suicide as a way of replacing the false self with the true.*

True self is the vital core of personality. Even when it is poorly developed and hidden under the facade of false self, it remains a reference mark by which a person judges himself and his life. Although true self has in common with false self a basis in social experience, there is a selfish, self-initiated, primitive quality in true self as contrasted to false self. When there is validation of a child's inclinations and his ways of expressing and implementing them, they become the basis of his identity. They become the warp into which his false (social) self can be woven. But when his inclinations have been discouraged he will not often act on them. He will tend to go along with his parents and identify himself in terms of his socially oriented behavior. Under such conditions there will be a split between his needs and his responses to others' needs. And in the more extreme case where he has been punished severely for expressing his needs, they will become unconscious. Then his social veneer, isolated from other parts of his personality, will be the only tangible sign to him of who he is. His self-image will have to be based on his veneer or on fantasy.

The worst kind of rearing, according to Winnicott, is an alternation of indulgence and exploitation in a tantalizingly irregular manner. The result is psychopathic behavior. Delinquents and psychopaths are people who have been indulged in infancy, then deprived and tantalized. They continue to operate on the expectation of receiving from the world, representing mother, things to which they feel still entitled. (It would seem that such an expectation motivates the quests of all heroes.)

Winnicott stressed temptation (rather than coercion) as the means by which mothers get infants to comply with their wishes. He and some writers cited in earlier chapters referred to "seductive" and "gratifying" parents, usually without specifying their meaning. It seems that sexual intercourse or petting is only rarely meant. Sometimes the meaning seems nonsexual, the gratifications consisting of food, toys, or attention. Most often something vaguely affectionate and sexual is indicated, consisting of any of the following: tender companionship with a romanticized aura of a lasting, exclusive relationship; body display and admiration; kissing, hugging, or caressing;

---

* According to Laing (1965), flagrant schizophrenia may constitute both a rebellion against mother and her substitutes in society and a search for one's true self.

erotic play centering around the bath or dressing; or sharing a bed. It is the incompletely defined middle area that usually concerns us, in which a relationship is implied, extending over periods of time between moments of arousal or gratification—an enduring relationship that is romanticized and eroticized. The main temptation offered the child is that the mother will be his exclusively and forever. The gratifications that reinforce this offer need not take any specific form; an occasional smile could serve as a reminder of the promise.

Temptation is more conducive to identity problems than is coercion. When a man reluctantly performs an act at gunpoint or under threat of injury, neither he nor his coercer are likely to have illusions about the act being willing, self-initiated, or, therefore, as representing the character of the doer. A child may accommodate a coercive mother as long as necessary, but he need not be misled as to his own motives. And his mother is not likely to be misled about the willingness of his behavior. Therefore she is not as likely to mislead him about it as when she perceives the initiative in his compliance to come from him.

Temptation, by contrast, implies a voluntary relationship. It means that desire is aroused in a person and that he therefore has difficulty in distinguishing between his own desire and that of the tempter. *Being manipulated to desire something results in another's motive being experienced as one's own, as if it originated in one's self.* Being tempted, therefore, fosters confusion about oneself. Where the induced desire is, in addition, a taboo one, there are further self-distorting effects. Anxiety, shame, and guilt are aroused as well as defense mechanisms which hide or disguise the forbidden desire, contributing to the development of mental disturbance. And when the taboo—the prohibition, punishment, or threat—arises from the same source as the desire, from the mother-temptress herself, we have a badly confusing situation for a child. A mother's wish for her son to be successful intellectually or in business may foster development of false self (i.e., patterns of behavior designed to bring her satisfaction), but will not in itself make him neurotic or psychotic. However, her desire that he be her lover may bring him into severe conflict. If she is sexually or affectionately inhibited, denies her demands, and punishes him for trying to fulfill them, then, according to Haley's (1963) analysis, he will respond by denying himself—denying that he is an active, responsible participant in the relationship. (Later he will deny himself in relation to other people.) In other words, demands for taboo behavior will foster disturbance as well as growth of false self. And, when the taboo is enforced by the person who is making the demands but who also denies making them, then the child is likely to show extreme denial of responsibility and identity.

NATURE AND CIVILIZATION

In view of the above hypotheses, an ideal rearing situation in relation to the development of identity is one in which sensitive, unselfish parents devote themselves to the needs of their babies during the early formative years, without interference or seriously conflicting interests. This ideal brings us to the old controversy about feeding infants on demand or on a schedule. A feeding schedule that goes by a clock—by any contingencies other than the infant's hunger—is an alienating condition to some extent. However, *a schedule that has been designed and adjusted to approximate his hunger rhythm is a schedule that is responsive to his needs.* And when such a schedule is modified toward the elimination of night feedings, not at some arbitrary age or solely because of the mother's fatigue, but in relation to the baby's increasing tendency to sleep through the night, such a modification is reasonably in tune with the baby's inclinations. (His sleeping more at night may reflect his physical maturation or learning of when his parents are more likely to respond to him.) The argument is not that parental needs are irrelevant, but that feeding can be scheduled in such a way that the infant is usually offered food when he feels hungry.

Toilet training, as it is usually done, is an essentially alienating process, reflecting primarily the interests of others. There is no toilet schedule that can approximate an infant's readiness to evacuate. And a one- or two-year-old child has no natural preference for using toilets as opposed to clothes or floors. In time he will acquire such a preference on the basis of imitation, encouragement, or coercion, but few parents wait for such a desire to develop to the point where training can proceed in response to the child's inclinations.

In general, home life is not a situation in which parents are free of competing demands during the time they give to their young children. Thus our hypotheses lead to the conclusion reached by Freud and other instinct-oriented theorists that the family as well as society are at odds with natural man and require the suppression of natural tendencies and their replacement by socially conditioned patterns of behavior. Growing up in the family means that, during the formative years, a child must accommodate to other people. And, as he begins to leave the home, his acceptance depends increasingly on subordinating his inclinations to schedules, rules, rites, and the needs and whims of others—teachers, friends, and other especially significant people. To the extent that these are inconsistent with his inclinations and impinge on him before his sense of self is established, culture is alienating.

However it does not follow that civilization is necessarily or greatly alienating. We may assume that a person with a clear sense of self and of his own ideas and interests need not find culture self-alienating; when he complies with demands of society that are inconsistent with his own inclinations, he will not confuse the two. This person, like one who is coerced, is not likely to make the mistake of thinking that what he does out of social convenience is a reflection of his individual desires or tastes. By contrast, a man who lacks a clear sense of himself and already confuses his social veneer with his individual inclinations may be further confused by new social demands. Social pressures would seem most alienating to those who are already alienated and to children whose sense of self is largely undeveloped.

How alienating social influences will be on a young child depends on how they fit with his individual inclinations. The development of true self or identity is fostered by social influences that recognize and are responsive to a child's inclinations. Whether a desire of his was inborn or newly acquired is not as important at any moment as whether it is recognized by others. Each experience can reinforce his desires as valid or can make them irrelevant to what happens. Toilet training will promote the development of a sense of self if it is done when the child feels an interest in it. It will be alienating if he participates in it to please his mother. It will be most alienating if, in addition, she tries to persuade him that he wants it. (His acquisition of an interest in toilet training may have been an alienating experience, or it may not. If it grew out of an interest in imitating someone whom he admires, no alienation need have been involved.)

Toilet training begun early to please parents is characteristic of our culture. Also typical is the increasing use of norms in child-rearing, and this too is an alienating influence insofar as mothers act on the basis of norms rather than in response to the individuality of their children. As averages are compiled on when babies smile, babble, eat specified foods, walk, speak, and develop various intellectual functions, these averages become demands. Parents seek guidelines from pediatricians and child-rearing manuals on when to do this and when to expect that of their babies, and guidelines are commonly given on the basis of averages. In addition, competitive discussion about babies' behavior is a common social activity of mothers, and boasting, exaggeration, and outright pretense result in mothers gaining distorted ideas about what the averages are. The interaction between mothering and infant norms appears to spiral upward; mothers with high expectations produce precocious babies, who raise the norms, which are then used by the next generation of mothers.

Civilization also spirals upward, as the contributions of one generation increase the opportunities the next generation will have and correspondingly increase the demands society will make. Gone are the days when only a handful were expected to contribute more than drudgery to the culture; high school graduates who go to college have passed the sixty percent mark. America at mid-century is a civilization in which women, nearing liberation, but still largely confined to low-status chores while their men go out and do what is prized in the culture, are in a particularly dissatisfied state. No longer content to be domestics nor yet ready for full rebellion, their situation is difficult, frustrating, and marked by largely suppressed resentment and ambition. Mothers' increasing dissatisfaction has made them more demanding of their sons and especially of their favorites. At the same time their frustration has hindered them from recognizing and meeting their sons' needs.

Besides the demands that mothers and others make of children, we are concerned with how those demands are implemented. Recent trends point toward increasing alienation from self, for seduction and manipulation have been replacing coercion in the rearing of children. The whip, rod, switch, and strap are relics of a bygone practice. The model mother of today, the proverbial "middle-class mother" (although found in every class), relies first on the offering and withholding of her love to motivate and discipline her children. Second she uses "reasoning" with them, which often means that she tries to persuade them that they want to do what, in fact, she wants them to do.

Similarly, teachers employ less naked power in dealing with pupils, but have more seductive and manipulative techniques available than before. The school more than any other institution is the promoter of the great society (which sounds temptingly like Eden) and of the almost unlimited opportunities which lie ahead for those who qualify. The school is the main stepping stone toward the future and, consequently, the main stumbling block. The teacher and the marks he gives determine to a large extent who will qualify. Recognizing these contingencies, students have adapted. As Friedenberg (1963) observed, we have developed a professional class of students: those who were committed to no values, facts, or theories, but were adept at sensing what their teachers wanted, even when those wants were unspoken, and at tailoring their performance accordingly.* In other words, we have gotten a body of students who are skilled at pleasing their teachers. When this skill is a subtle one—when the student reads his teacher's implicit cues and disguises his sycophancy by what passes for scholarship, and when this occurs in the context of parental and societal ambitions for children and the competitiveness of our culture —then both student and teacher may mistake the student's performance to be a reflection of his own inclination.

THE BORED SOCIETY

Psychopaths are not the only ones plagued by monotony. Parents are surprised by children who complain that they have nothing to do. Today's children have so much more than their parents did in terms of activities, toys, and television that it seems perverse of them to be bored. The multitude of external stimulants available to children emphasizes the lack of inner stimulation in those who seem to get bored quickly.

Besides children, many adults find their lives monotonous. And the lives of many more are enlivened chiefly by activities designed to prevent monotony. To a substantial extent our culture is based on fear of boredom. Escapism in recreation has long been noted in American culture, and it is on the increase. The omnipresent television was an addition to our already heavy consumption of titillating reading, movies, and spectator sports. And while there was concern that home viewing would reduce the use of other amusements, the opposite seems to have occurred. Book sales multiplied during the television era, as

---

* A striking revelation in the Watergate scandal was that very bright young men reacted instantly to their leaders' unspoken interests; without instruction and with little hesitancy they engaged in elaborate illegal activities in their leaders' behalf.

The newer trend among students to demand consideration of their wishes by teachers and schools is limited to a minority, and it remains to be seen if the majority will reverse their adaptation.

did major professional sports franchises and attendance. And movies, after a shaky period, increased their audience by offering more sexual titillation.

We all know people who are distressed when they lack scheduled activity. Holding a second job used to be a reflection of economic need, but now men take second and even third jobs in the absence of necessity, and women go to work out of boredom. Many people with minor illness do not enjoy their opportunity to relax; rather, they fret and are unpleasant to have around. Enforced retirement is dreaded and sometimes fatal.

Gifts are an increasingly used means of making routine events exciting. If a woman needs a household appliance, instead of making a purchase she asks her husband for one. He then can "give" it to her. By this device, he shows that he is generous and concerned about her, and she receives a gift and expresses gratitude. Something out of the ordinary has happened.

Gifts in childhood were exciting things which made holidays stand out. They served to show us how well we were thought of or loved, especially if we had parents who did not express sentiment in more personal ways. Adults, especially affluent ones, can simply buy things for themselves. But that gives limited satisfaction. A man who wants a set of golf clubs which he considers too expensive may let his wife know his wish. Then she can buy it for him (and charge it). He will have the clubs as a gift, although he will pay no less when he pays the bill. He may pay the additional price of getting a set which is not the one he wants and of keeping it in order not to offend her. But he has the gift as a token from her. People give themselves gifts also. A woman may want a garment, say she cannot afford it, and then decide to make herself a present of it.

Such mental manipulations are more than rationales to justify acquiring things. Pretending that we cannot afford something gives it more than ordinary meaning. The ritual implies that the gift was valuable and unavailable or even forbidden, with the excitement that accompanies taboo gratification. Getting something undeserved can be intoxicating, suggesting that we are in the lap of Fortune.

Scarcity is a way of life for Americans according to Slater (1970). Despite the affluence of our country, we operate on the assumption that there is not enough to satisfy human needs. Therefore "people must compete with one another for . . . scarce resources—lie, swindle, steal, and kill if necessary." Military budgets and corruption lend credibility to the illusion of scarcity by draining off some of the abundance. Our vital public services (schools, hospitals) skimp regularly and go from one financial crisis to another.

Apprehension of scarcity creates tension in otherwise casual undertakings. Competition makes human interaction dramatic, and crises mobilize people. Vicarious participation in staged spectacle excites us. Thus our way of life counters the lack of inner stimulation, the threat of boredom. It provides us with frequent injections of adrenalin. Our historical policy of international isolationism, with occasional military adventures, has been replaced by a posture of world leadership and an attempt to impose our kind of peace. The result is frequent involvement in warfare, and war is a well established distraction from a condition of alienation.

The idea that vital resources are insufficient for human needs is more obviously an illusion when applied to resources that are virtually inexhaustible, like love and sex. Love does not deplete a lover, and the common idea that a mother, for example, has a fixed quantity of it to distribute among her husband and children is not based on fact. If anything, the contrary seems likely; one loving experience increases the possibility for another. Sometimes the scarcity of love is the result of deliberate manipulation, as when a parent rations it to discipline a child. Thus many mothers give their children the impression that love is scarce and sometimes unattainable, and that they must earn it or compete for it. The taboo on mother-son love adds to its apparent scarcity. Sex is similarly treated as in short supply. The traditional idea of virginity as a precious gift which can be given only once symbolizes our scarcity outlook and hoarding reaction. Boys grow up with so strong a sense of the scarcity of sex that no matter how abundant they find it in one adult relationship they will be tempted by the possibility of another. The experience of past deprivation and the expectation of it in the future, plus the taboo on sex, combine to produce a hunger for it which is never satisfied. This hunger is always available to advertisers who use seductive women to sell all kinds of products and services.

Behind the scarcity philosophy seems to be the idea that man is like a mule. He is seen as having so little inner drive that without deprivation behind him, tantalization in front, and the whip of crises on both sides, he will lie down and civilization will come to an end.

Thus the view of man as alienated from his needs and interests is used to justify treating him in ways that alienate him further.

Dedication is another way of combatting the fear of apathetic inactivity. People instruct and threaten themselves; they make bargains with God and give pledges to almost anyone. A person's uncertainty about his identity and what he should do can be resolved by his throwing himself into a role or mission. "He needs me" is a declaration which sustains many people in relationships that have limited possibilities: a child devoting himself to a sick parent; an adult to an unloved spouse; and, of course, a parent to a child. Alienation is an obstacle to deep love; the expectation of disappointment is another. Romantic infatuation used to be a more acceptable alternative to love, but it has limited appeal. Infatuation is thought to make a person weak, helpless, and vulnerable. And alienated people are wary of vulnerability; they seek power as a means of being recognized and belonging. "He needs me" does not endanger one's power base, but adds to it.

When one is not a part of anything, "I need you" can be a cry to belong, a plea for acceptance. The plea would seem to imply exposing oneself as weak. But helplessness and personal commitment are more apparent than real in most dependent relationships among adults. That is, many dependent people are highly manipulative of those on whom they depend and covertly find their sense of power enhanced in the relationships. In addition, "I need him" is usually an attitude with little passion; "I need Al" is readily replaced by "I need Bill." One does not have to suffer bereavement of the first nor fall in love with the second in order to make the transfer. Therefore dependency is possible for many alienated people.

A woman's role used to be determined largely by her marital status, and her husband's name was a significant part of her identity. But marriage is becoming a feeble ceremony; it fails increasingly to metamorphose people's identity. The role of wife without children is relatively meaningless for many. However, alienated women can orient their lives to a large extent by a mother-child relationship. Childbirth is a powerful experience; it is probably the most potent initiation of all. For many women the agony of labor and delivery reaches the limit of human endurance. Their unconsciousness or twilight sleep is marked by dreams of mysterious things happening to them. And the newborn infant evokes images which are wonderful and grotesque; he may be seen as God's child or as an evil, animalistic monster. Thus the initiatory stages of death, change, and birth are starkly present in childbirth, and contribute to the new identity which women find in motherhood.

Experiencing one's child as a gift, especially a gift from God, enhances the role of motherhood. The first year in the child's life is often reported to be the most glorious in the mother's. The barriers of alienated women fall and they envelop their babies with a passion which their husbands or lovers will never know. Need and mutual dependency are so marked in these relationships that they have been called symbiotic.

The infant's maturation brings changes. When the relationship can no longer be summed up by "He needs me," mothers become ambivalent. Particularly disturbing to many is the emergence of sexual interests in their sons. Besdine (1968), Olmsted (1962), and many others report withdrawal by mothers beginning as infancy ends. In addition we may conjecture about nonsexual reasons for maternal ambivalence. An infant is a thing; in many ways it strikes people as not quite human. And some people relate more comfortably to things than to people. But a child of several years is definitely human. He is capable of demanding an interpersonal relationship of some depth and maturity. And an alienated woman who has not related in a mature way to her husband is not likely to do so with her child either. A child of several years is also capable of seriously disappointing her. Therefore the older he gets the more vulnerable she will be if she remains close and open to him. Perhaps she will anticipate his growing away and leaving her, and she may withdraw to insulate herself against anticipated loss.

In any case, the growing up of their children is traumatic for many women. For some the crisis comes when a child enters school; for others, when he leaves home. And the crisis is one of identity. Those who have defined themselves in terms of motherhood become confused and depressed. If the role of mother is the only one they are prepared to play, they are likely to flounder when no one needs them to play it.

For alienated men, job or career serves as the primary source of identity. Some men who lose their jobs become lost people, whose despair makes their families miserable. To be typed in a role that ceases to exist contributes to feeling unnecessary and useless. The feeling then leads to wanting to be needed, and the cycle may begin again.

THE ROAD TO PARADISE

Psychologists have portrayed the baby who is mothered excessively as living in a paradise where he is king. The idea that a newborn can comprehend such a situation and later wish to return to it is fanciful. But it is meaningful to say that gratification early in life can be a factor in maintaining adult behavior. As conditioning studies have shown, preliminary basic gratification can make token rewards effective in maintaining behavior over long periods of time.

A baby who is mostly cared for by one person becomes highly dependent upon her. In the first half year of life he will prefer her over others to be near him and may be upset if her appearance is changed, as by her using unfamiliar facial expressions or sounds. In the second half year he may react to strangers with crying and signs of fear, and to his mother's prolonged absence by massive disturbance in his behavior. In these terms we may say that he develops a close bond to her.

For Jocasta's chosen child, the bond is greater than usual. He is born into an unreal paradise—one constructed out of the frustrations of his mother. More than most mothers and infants, the two of them live alone in their Eden, even at times to the physical exclusion of husband and other children. They look to each other for all gratification. Such a mother, wanting the relationship to continue indefinitely, transmits that expectation to the child, and then fails to live up to it. His Eden, an arbitrary creation of her fantasies, can be taken from him at any time, and as the months go by it is taken away for any number of reasons. Besides her being disappointed in him or upset by his demands, the birth of a new child or separation occasioned by illness may interfere with their closeness. Whatever the reason, the child's paradise becomes a lost one, and he tends thereafter to struggle to regain it, with intermittent encouragement from her. Some children search for the rest of their lives, channeling their efforts into socially valued pursuits like success in the arts or sports or the salvation of their fellow men. Others give up some parts of the dream, disguise other parts, and pursue a symbolic substitute for Eve in Eden, as at the gambling table. Still others drop out of the chase entirely.

Whatever chosen children do in pursuit of paradise is likely to be alienating, whether it is learning to use the toilet or to sing, to the extent that they are following a script written by another. The harder they follow the dream, the more self-alienated they become. The harder they work at their calling, the more they lose themselves.

The chosen one is not the master of his life nor even of many of his fantasies. Our dreams are considered to be the result of frustrated, repressed, or otherwise unexpressed desires. Thus they represent our inner selves. When Jocasta dreams of a lover or champion, a gifted child who will be an extension of herself, the dream is presumably her own, born of the bitter disappointments in her life. But when her son dreams of being that champion, he is dreaming her dream. Thus even his private, silent mental processes are not much his own, except for the dream of a return to an infantile paradise. Because his dream of becoming a hero is not his own, he cannot find fulfillment in his climb toward greatness, nor can he find himself in it.

"Alienation is intimately associated with man's compulsion to achieve the impossible," said Van Bark (1961). She compared modern alienated man to the figure in a great many myths and stories who denies or sells a part of himself in return for special powers, but becomes a slave in the process. In modern times, selling one's identity would correspond to the selling of one's soul. One who has, as a child, oriented himself around his parent's wishes by suppressing his own, grows into manhood striving to return to a lost paradise, but often feeling powerless to achieve that or any other meaningful goal. He is a likely candidate to sell himself further, to shape his personality to the whims of those who promise him special recognition, position, or power. He wants the power to enable him to win his divine bride and to enter paradise, but the more he tries, the more lonely and abject a stranger he becomes.

BIBLIOGRAPHY

ADLER, A. "Billy the Kid." In *Western Folklore*, 1951, *10*, 143–52.

ALBEE, E. *The Zoo Story*. New York: Coward-McCann, 1960.

ARENDT, H. *The Human Condition*. Chicago: University of Chicago Press, 1958.

ARISTOTLE. *Politics*. New York: Modern Library, 1943.

BACON, F. "Of Great Place." In *Bacon's Essays*. Boston: Little Brown, 1891.

BEALL, L. "The Dynamics of Suicide." In *Bulletin of Suicidology*, March 1969.

BELLOW, S. *Dangling Man*. New York: Vanguard, 1944.

BERGLER, E. *The Psychology of Gambling*. New York: Hill and Wang, 1957.

———. "Psychopathic personalities are unconsciously propelled by a defense against a specific type of psychic masochism—'malignant masochism.'" In *Archives of Criminal Psychodynamics*, 1961, *4*, 416–34.

BESDINE, M. "Jocasta and Oedipus." In *Pathways in Child Guidance*, March 1968.

———. "Mrs. Oedipus." In *Psychology Today*, January 1969.

———. "Jewish Mothering." In *Jewish Spectator*, February 1970.

BLANCHE, E. E. "Gambling Odds are Gimmicked!" In *Annals of Amer. Acad. of Political and Social Science*. #269, May 1950.

BRODEY, W. M. "Some Family Operations and Schizophrenia." In *Archives of General Psychiatry*, 1959, *1*, 379–402.

BROMBERG, W. "The Psychopathic Personality Concept Re-evaluated." In *Archives of Criminal Psychodynamics*, 1961, *4*, 435–42.

BROWN, N. O. *Hermes, the Thief*. Madison: University of Wisconsin Press, 1947.

CAMPBELL, J. *The Hero with a Thousand Faces*. Cleveland: Meridian, 1956.

CLECKLEY, H. *The Mask of Sanity*. St. Louis: Mosby, 1941 (1st ed.), 1964 (4th ed.).

DEUTSCH, H. *Neuroses and Character Types*. New York: International Universities, 1965.

——. *Psychoanalytic Study of the Myth of Dionysus and Apollo*. New York: International Universities, 1969.

EHRENBERG, V. "Sophoclean Rulers: Oedipus." In O'Brien, M. J., ed., *Twentieth Century Interpretations of Oedipus Rex*. Englewood Cliffs, N.J.: Prentice-Hall, Spectrum Books, 1968.

ELIADE, M. *Rites and Symbols of Initiation*. New York: Harper Torchbooks, 1965.

ELLISON, R. W. *Invisible Man*. New York: Signet, 1953.

EMERSON, R. W. "Lecture on the Times." In *Representative Men; Nature, Addresses and Lectures*. Philadelphia: McKay, 1892.

FARBEROW, N. L., and SHNEIDMAN, E. S. *The Cry for Help*. New York: McGraw-Hill, 1961.

FENICHEL, O. *The Psychoanalytic Theory of Neurosis*. New York: Norton, 1945.

FERGUSSON, F. *The Idea of a Theater*. Princeton: Princeton University Press, 1949.

FEUER, L. S. *The Conflict of Generations*. New York: Basic Books, 1969.

FORER, L. K. *Birth Order and Life Roles*. Springfield, Ill.: Thomas, 1969.

FRAZER, J. G. *The Golden Bough*, abridged ed. New York: Macmillan, 1940.

FREUD, S. "Dostoevsky and Parricide." In *Collected Papers*, Vol. 5. New York: Basic Books, 1959.

FRIEDENBERG, E. Z. *Coming of Age in America*. New York: Vintage Books, 1963.

FROMM, E. *The Sane Society*. New York: Rinehart, 1955.

FROMM-REICHMANN, F. "Loneliness." In *Psychiatry*, 1959, *22*, 1–15.

GALDSTON, I. "The Gambler and His Love." In Herman, R. D., ed., *Gambling*. New York: Harper and Row, 1967.

Gamblers Anonymous. Los Angeles: Gamblers Anonymous Publishing Company, 1964.

GEHA, R. "Dostoevsky and 'The Gambler.'" In *Psychoanalytic Review*, 1970, *57*, 95–123, 289–302.

GILBERT, G. M. "Hermann Goering, Amiable Psychopath." In *Journ. of Abnormal and Social Psychology*, 1948, *43*, 211–29.

GOODMAN, P. *Growing Up Absurd*. New York: Vintage Books, 1960.

————. "Youth Subculture and an Unteachable Generation." In Wertheimer, M., ed., *Confrontation*. Glenview, Ill.: Scott Foresman, 1970.

GORDONE, C. *No Place to Be Somebody*. Indianapolis: Bobbs-Merrill, 1969.

GORER, G. "British Life—It's a Gamble." In Herman, R. D., ed., *Gambling*. New York: Harper and Row, 1967.

GREEN, A. W. "The Middle-Class Male Child and Neurosis." In *Amer. Sociological Review*, 1946, *11*, 31–41.

GREENACRE, P. "Conscience in the Psychopath." In *Amer. Journ. of Orthopsychiatry*, 1945, *15*, 495–509.

————. *Trauma, Growth and Personality*. New York: Norton, 1952.

————. "Problems of Patient-Therapist Relationship in the Treatment of Psychopaths." In Lindner, R. M., and Seliger, R. V., *Handbook of Correctional Psychology*. New York: Philosophical Library, 1947.

GREENSON, R. R. "On Gambling." In *Amer. Imago*, 1947, *4*, 61–77.

HALEY, J. *Strategies of Psychotherapy*. New York: Grune and Stratton, 1963.

HALLECK, S. L. *Psychiatry and the Dilemma of Crime*. New York: Hoeber, 1967.

HARE, R. D. *Psychopathy*. New York: Wiley, 1970.

HARRIS, H. I. "Gambling Addiction in an Adolescent Male." In *Psychoanalytic Quarterly*, 1964, *33*, 513–25.

HEAVER, W. L. "A Study of Forty Male Psychopathic Personalities Before, During and After Hospitalization." In *Amer. Journ. of Psychiatry*, 1943, *100*, 342–46.

HENDERSON, D. K. *Psychopathic States*. New York: Norton, 1939.

HENDIN, H. *Black Suicide*. New York: Basic Books, 1969.

HOFFMAN, W. S. *The Loser*. New York: Funk and Wagnalls, 1968.

JOHNSON, A. M., and SZUREK, S. A. "The Genesis of Antisocial Acting Out in Children and Adults." In *Psychoanalytic Quarterly*, 1952, *21*, 323–43.

KENISTON, K. *The Uncommitted*. New York: Harcourt Brace Jovanovich, 1965.

————. *Young Radicals*. New York: Harcourt Brace Jovanovich, 1968.

KESEY, K. *One Flew Over the Cuckoo's Nest*. New York: Viking, 1962.

KIRKWOOD, G. M. *A Study of Sophoclean Drama*. Ithaca: Cornell University Press, 1958.

KLAPP, O. E. *Collective Search for Identity*. New York: Holt, Rinehart and Winston, 1969.

KOZOL, H. L. "The Dynamics of Psychopathy." In *Archives of Criminal Psychodynamics*, 1961, *4*, 526–41.

LAING, R. D. *The Divided Self*. Baltimore: Penguin, 1965.

LEVY, D. M. "The Deprived and Indulged Forms of Psychopathic Personality." In *Amer. Journ. of Orthopsychiatry*, 1951, *21*, 250–54.

LEVY-BRUHL, L. "Primitive Mentality and Gambling." In *Criterion*, 1924, *2*, 188–200.

LINDNER, R. M.   *Rebel Without a Cause.* New York: Grune and Stratton, 1944.

——.   "The Psychodynamics of Gambling." In *Annals of Amer. Acad. of Political and Social Science,* #269, May 1950, 93–107.

LUDOVICI, L. J.   *The Itch for Play.* London: Jarrolds, 1962.

MACHIAVELLI, N.   *The Prince.* New York: Modern Library, 1940.

MACIVER, R. M.   *The Ramparts We Guard.* New York: Macmillan, 1950.

MARX, K.   *Economic and Philosophical Manuscripts of 1884.* New York: International, 1964.

MASTERS, R. E. L.   *Patterns of Incest.* New York: Julian, 1963.

MAURER, D. W.   "The Argot of the Dice Gambler." In *Annals of Amer. Acad. of Political and Social Science,* #269, May 1950, 114–33.

MAY, R.   *Man's Search for Himself.* New York: Norton, 1953.

McCORD, W., and McCORD, J.   *The Psychopath.* Princeton: Van Nostrand, 1964.

McKERRACHER, D. W., LOUGHNANE, T., and WATSON, R. A.   "Self-mutilation in Female Psychopaths." In *British Journ. of Psychiatry,* 1968, *114,* 829–32.

MENNINGER, K. A.   *Man Against Himself.* New York: Harcourt Brace Jovanovich, 1938.

MERTON, R. K.   *Social Theory and Social Structure,* 2nd ed. New York: Free Press, 1957.

NORMAN, D.   *The Hero.* New York: World, 1969.

O'BRIEN, M. J.   "Introduction." In *Twentieth Century Interpretations of Oedipus Rex.* Englewood Cliffs, N.J.: Prentice-Hall, Spectrum Books, 1968.

OLMSTED, C.   *Heads I Win Tails You Lose.* New York: Macmillan, 1962.

PEARSON, K.   *The Chances of Death,* Vol. 1. London: Arnold, 1897.

POINSETT, A.   "Tragedy of a Compulsive Gambler." In *Ebony,* December 1965.

QUAY, H. C.   "Psychopathic Personality as Pathological Stimulation-seeking." In *Amer. Journ. of Psychiatry,* 1965, *122,* 180–83.

RADIN, P.   *The Trickster.* New York: Schocken, 1972.

RAGLAN, F. R. S.   *The Hero.* London: Watts, 1949.

RANK, O.   *The Myth of the Birth of the Hero.* New York: Vintage Books, 1959.

REINER, B. S., and KAUFMAN, I.   *Character Disorders in Parents of Delinquents.* New York: Family Service Ass'n. of America, 1959.

RICHARDSON, J.   "Grace through Gambling." In *Esquire,* April 1967.

ROBERTSON, J. G.   "Eulenspiegel, Till." In *Encyclopaedia Britannica,* 14th ed., 1940.

ROBINS, E.   "Antisocial and Dyssocial Personality Disorders." In Freedman, A. M., and Kaplan, H. I., eds., *Comprehensive Handbook of Psychiatry.* Baltimore: Williams and Wilkins, 1967.

ROIPHE, A. R. "The Family Is Out of Fashion." In *New York Times Magazine,* August 15, 1971.

ROSEN, E., and GREGORY, I. *Abnormal Psychology.* Philadelphia: Saunders, 1965.

ROSENTHAL, R., and JACOBSON, L. *Pygmalion in the Classroom.* New York: Holt, Rinehart and Winston, 1968.

ROSNER, S. "Problems of Working-through with Borderline Patients." In *Psychotherapy,* 1969, *6,* 43–45.

ROSTEN, L. C. "The Adoration of the Nag." In Herman, R. D., ed., *Gambling.* New York: Harper and Row, 1967.

RUITENBEEK, H. M. *The Individual and the Crowd.* New York: Mentor, 1965.

SARTRE, J. P. "Dirty Hands." In *Three Plays.* New York: Knopf, 1949.

SAUER, G. "Introduction." In Shaw, G., *Meat on the Hoof.* New York: St. Martins, 1972.

SEEMAN, M. "On the Meaning of Alienation." In *Amer. Sociological Review,* 1959, *24,* 783–91.

SHAW, G. *Meat on the Hoof.* New York: St. Martins, 1972.

SLATER, P. E. *The Pursuit of Loneliness.* Boston: Beacon, 1970.

————. *The Glory of Hera.* Boston: Beacon, 1971.

SLOCHOWER, H. "The Juvenile Delinquent and the Mythic Hero." In *Dissent,* 1961, *8,* 413–18.

STOPPARD, T. *Rosencrantz and Guildenstern Are Dead.* New York: Grove, 1967.

SUNDBERG, N. D., and TYLER, L. E. *Clinical Psychology.* New York: Appleton-Century-Crofts, 1962.

SZUREK, S. A. "Notes on the Genesis of Psychopathic Personality Trends." In *Psychiatry,* 1942, *5,* 1–6.

TEITELBAUM, S. H. "The Psychopathic Style of Life and Its Defensive Function." In *Amer. Journ. of Psychotherapy,* 1965, *19,* 126–36.

THORNE, F. C. "The Etiology of Sociopathic Reactions." In Rabkin, L. Y., and Carr, J. E., eds., *Sourcebook in Abnormal Psychology.* New York: Houghton Mifflin, 1967.

TINDER, G. *The Crisis of Political Imagination.* New York: Scribners, 1964.

TOMAN, W. *Family Constellation,* 2nd ed. New York: Springer, 1969.

TRILLING, L. *Freud and the Crisis of Our Culture.* Boston: Beacon, 1955.

TRIPPETT, F. "The Suckers." In *Look,* May 19, 1970.

TURGENEV, I. "The Diary of a Superfluous Man." In *The Borzoi Turgenev.* New York: Knopf, 1950.

URICK, R. V. *Alienation.* Englewood Cliffs, N.J.: Prentice-Hall, 1970.

VAN BARK, B. S. "The Alienated Person in Literature." In *Amer. Journ. of Psychoanalysis,* 1961, *21,* 183–93.

WATTS, A.   *The Book.* New York: Pantheon, 1956.

WEISS, J. M. A.   "The Gamble with Death in Attempted Suicide." In *Psychiatry*, 1957, *20*, 17–25.

WHEELIS, A.   *The Quest for Identity.* New York: Norton, 1958.

WILSON, C.   *Ritual in the Dark.* New York: Houghton Mifflin, 1960.

WINNICOTT, D. W.   *Collected Papers.* New York: Basic Books, 1958.

————.   *The Maturational Processes and the Facilitating Environment.* New York: International Universities, 1965.

WINNINGTON-INGRAM, R. P.   "The *Oedipus Tyrannus* and Greek Archaic Thought." In O'Brien, M. J., ed., *Twentieth Century Interpretations of Oedipus Rex.* Englewood Cliffs, N.J.: Prentice-Hall, Spectrum Books, 1968.

WOLFE, T.   *Look Homeward, Angel.* New York: Scribners, 1929.

Index

143